ESSAYS AND STUDIES
1978

ESSAYS AND STUDIES
1978

BEING VOLUME THIRTY-ONE OF THE NEW SERIES
OF ESSAYS AND STUDIES COLLECTED FOR
THE ENGLISH ASSOCIATION

BY W. W. ROBSON

JOHN MURRAY

FIFTY ALBEMARLE STREET LONDON

Printed in Great Britain by
Cox & Wyman Ltd, London, Fakenham and Reading

0 7195 3506 9

Contents

I

'Rooteles moot grene soone deye': The Helplessness of Chaucer's Troilus and Criseyde

COLIN MANLOVE

THOUGH much excellent work has been done on the failure of perspective in the love of Chaucer's Troilus and Criseyde, most of it tends to be concerned with the lack of vision and of philosophic and religious detachment in the lovers.[1] While mentioning this aspect as part of the amorous myopia portrayed, this article will also discuss the way in which Troilus and Criseyde become dissociated from the mundane world and thereby unable to influence its alterations: for Chaucer's vision of the fatal possibilities in making human love a final value stems not only from a religious standpoint but also from a social, moral and practical one. Absence of worldly sense, passivity, and the assertion of private values over public are the themes that will most concern us: they are only in part metaphors for the lack of religious vision, for Chaucer is as concerned in this poem with secular standards of conduct as with life as a pilgrimage to final judgment.

Having fallen in love with Criseyde, Troilus first abandons all other concerns for her, and later bases them on her.

> So muche, day by day, his owene thought
> For lust to hire, gan quiken and encresse
> That every other charge he sette at nought. (1.442–4)[2]

Chaucer takes pains to emphasize this, telling us that Troilus was no longer troubled by the siege of Troy (463–4) and that

---

[1] See e.g. D. W. Robertson, Jr., A Preface to Chaucer (Princeton, New Jersey, 1962), pp. 472 ff; less extreme are Ida L. Gordon, The Double Sorrow of Troilus (Oxford, 1970) and P. M. Kean, Chaucer and the Making of English Poetry Volume 1: Love Vision and Debate (1972), pp. 112–78.

[2] References throughout are to F. N. Robinson, ed., The Works of Geoffrey Chaucer (2nd ed., 1957).

> The sharp shoures of armes preve,
> That Ector or his othere brethren diden,
> Ne made hym only therfore ones meve. (470–2)

Troilus does still go to battle, and performs wondrous feats of arms,

> But for non hate he to the Grekes hadde,
> Ne also for the rescous of the town,
> Ne made hym thus in armes for to madde,
> But only, lo, for this conclusioun:
> To liken hire the bet for his renoun. (477–81)

For a time he is incapacitated by the torment of his love, and feigns physical sickness in order to keep to his bed of passive lamentation (484–91). However, when he has confessed his love to Pandarus, and has been promised help, he can go forth again. He becomes the terror of the Greeks and the moral cynosure of Troy, 'That ecch hym loved that loked on his face':

> For he bicom the frendlieste wight,
> The gentilest, and ek the mooste fre,
> The thriftiest and oon the beste knyght,
> That in his tyme was or myghte be.
> Dede were his japes and his cruelte,
> His heighe port and his manere estraunge,
> And ecch of tho gan for a vertu chaunge. (1079–85)

This transformation is dilated upon at the end of Book III (1772–1806). Yet Chaucer stresses its source: 'This encrees of hardynesse and myght/Com him of love, his ladies thank to wynne,/That altered his spirit so withinne' (1776–8). What comes first is Criseyde, not Troy; love, not virtue.[1] When he hears of Pandarus' success with Criseyde, Troilus can declare, '"A thousand Troyes whoso that me yave,/ Ech after other, God so wys me save,/Ne myghte me so gladen"' (II.977–9). When Troilus is expecting to

[1] See also Robertson, p. 478.

meet Criseyde in secret, he covers his tracks by putting out the story that if he is missed he has gone to the temple of Apollo to learn in holy solitude from the god 'next whan Grekes sholde flee' (III.544). Chaucer makes us distinctly aware of a dangerous absolutism and lack of perspective in Troilus' behaviour: the experience of love is near joy itself, and its products the centre of mortal worth, yet it cannot be the sole arbiter of behaviour.

This limitation of perspective is seen in other areas. We are continually reminded that the love Troilus and Criseyde share is governed by the mutable character of fortune.[1] It is thus that Troilus experiences love when he is first smitten by Criseyde. He switches between joy and despair, describing his plight in terms of the standard image of fortune as stormy sea, with himself a rudderless boat upon it:

> 'Thus possed to and fro,
> Al stereles withinne a boot am I
> Amydde the see, bitwixen wyndes two,
> That in contrarie stonden evere mo.
> Allas! what is this wondre maladie?
> For hete of cold, for cold of hete, I dye.' (I.415–20)

Criseyde, too, experiences the same oscillations of feeling as she begins to love Troilus (II.806–12). She is acutely aware of the unstable character of love's joys before she enters into them:

> 'For love is yet the mooste stormy lyf,
> Right of hymself, that evere was bigonne;
> For evere som mystrust or nice strif
> There is in love, som cloude is over that sonne.' (II.778–81)

When Criseyde understands that Troilus believes she has been false with Horaste, she is quick to expatiate on the transitory character of worldly joy, '"O brotel wele of mannes joie unstable!"' (III.813–40); and again when she hears the news of her impending exchange for Antenor, '"Endeth thanne love in wo?

[1] On this and Boethian elements in the poem see also Robertson, pp. 472–4, 477–9, 494; Gordon, pp. 24–60; Kean, loc. cit., passim.

Ye, or men lieth!"' (IV.834–40). Even at the height of their bliss the lovers know the uncertain character of their experience:

> lo, this was hir moste feere,
> That al this thyng but nyce dremes were;
> For which ful ofte ech of hem seyde, 'O swete,
> Clippe ich yow thus, or elles I it meete?' (III.1341–4)

Yet while such knowledge invites, it does not produce detachment. When Troilus hears of the exchange he asks fortune what he has done to deserve this (IV.260–80), quite forgetting that it is fortune's nature to betray and to act without regard to the merit of those who subject themselves to her sway.[1] Chaucer gives us the perspective the lovers refuse: 'thus Fortune a tyme ledde in joie/Criseyde, and ek this kynges sone of Troie' (III.1714–15); and

> But al to litel, weylaway the whyle,
> Lasteth swich joie, ythonked be Fortune,
> That semeth trewest whan she wol bygyle,
> And kan to fooles so hire song entune,
> That she hem hent and blent, traitour commune!
> And whan a wight is from hire whiel ythrowe,
> Than laugheth she, and maketh hym the mowe.
>   (IV.1–7; see also V.469, 1134, 1541–54)

The suggestion of a dimension that has been lost, even while the losing it produces so magnificent a love, is inescapable. And much the same is true of the philosophic and religious perspective continually suggested by the poem: of which more later.

Perhaps the central image in the poem of the restriction of the lovers' purview, and of their disengagement from the world, is Pandarus. It is Pandarus who has all the dealings with the world required for the success of the love, and he who makes it possible for Troilus and Criseyde to be wholly passive (Diomede needs no such intermediary).[2] The very existence of Pandarus is a constant

---

[1] Cf. Boethius, *De Consolatione Philosophiae*, IV. Pr. 2.

[2] John Lawlor, *Chaucer* (1968), p. 53 asks, 'Without Pandarus, what should these two *know* of love, let alone advance to its fulfilment?'

reminder of the severance of the lovers from the public world, and of their failure to impose their wills on circumstances. And as Pandarus goes to work, arranging matters, making practical suggestions, tempering excessive feelings with homely advice and generally taking a more 'realistic' and earthy view of love, we see that he offers and orchestrates a commonsense approach to experience which the lovers are without. His vision cannot contain the heights of love to which Troilus and Criseyde reach, and there is perhaps no compromise between his *Weltanschauung* and theirs, but we are nevertheless made clearly aware through him of a larger context and a rational mode of behaviour which his charges lack.

Pandarus is the vessel of the free will, activity and engagement abandoned by Troilus and Criseyde. All that the lovers have to do is love: Pandarus, and to a small extent fate, do the acting to bring them together. Of course the passivity is more obvious in the case of Troilus: with Criseyde it is a case of enforced helplessness, whereby Pandarus manipulates her into loving Troilus. She does indeed love Troilus, and out of some free choice, when he has been put in the most favourable light by Pandarus and by fate (in his riding by at a critical moment), but the love remains a manipulated one.

In Book I Pandarus wrings from Troilus both the fact that he loves and the identity of his beloved; and calms Troilus by giving him hope of success. In Book II Pandarus manages Criseyde, first, by holding her in suspense as to the news he has for her, and then, having revealed it, by immediately threatening his own and Troilus' deaths if she will not yield (II.323 ff.). Then he caters for her female caution by saying that he is not asking her to give herself wholly to Troilus, but only to '"make hym bettre chiere"' (351–64); and follows this up with assurances that the people of Troy will not lewdly misconstrue any visits to her by Troilus, and with *carpe diem* injunctions (365–406). On Criseyde's complaint of Pandarus' falseness to her, the threats of instant death are renewed, and Criseyde, 'which that wel neigh starf for feere' (449) resolves to temporize, '"myn herte ayeins my lust [to] constreyne"' (476). To give herself some ground to go on, she asks Pandarus to tell her how he first learnt of Troilus' love, and whether Troilus can '"wel speke of love"' (499–504). Pandarus thus has the opportunity to put Troilus in a very favourable light, and though Criseyde instantly denounces his concluding prayer that '"ye ben his al hool, as he is youre,"' the character of Troilus is securely lodged in her mind; and the rather puzzled stanza (603–9), in which she says that though Troilus love her, there is no need for her to love him, suggests how she has been knocked away from certainty. At this point, by the one pure accident in the poem—presented, interestingly, without any mention of fate or destinal purpose— Troilus himself rides by in all his martial glory, and Criseyde has her first sight of him, at which she begins to be transformed ('"Who yaf me drynke?"'). She now explores a variety of reasons, amorous, politic and vainglorious for giving favour to Troilus; slips back into fear of the constraints and possible miseries of love, and revives once more on hearing Antigone her niece sing the praises of love and its effects, to the extent that she 'wex somwhat able to converte' (694–902).

Meanwhile Pandarus tells Troilus to ride by Criseyde's house next day, and instructs him in the writing of a love-letter, even down to the detail of blotting it with his tears. Pandarus takes the letter to Criseyde and persuades her into accepting it; she writes her cautious reply. Pandarus tricks her into being seated by the window when Troilus appears, and stops her flight: she becomes further attracted to him. Thus matters remain for a time, with further exchanges of letters and occasional glimpses, all managed by Pandarus. Pandarus' next move is to arrange a meeting between the lovers, and he does this by the deception, practised on both Criseyde and Troilus' brothers, that one Poliphete is seeking to damage her position in Troy, and that she needs help against him: he has her come to the house of Deiphebus to put her position, and arranges matters so that Troilus, whose help she will also have to solicit, will be feigning sickness in a small room of the house. In this way, Troilus can declare his love, and Criseyde accepts his service. Pandarus then plots a more intimate meeting between the two in his own house. He pretends to Criseyde that Troilus is out of town in order to persuade her to come to supper at his house. Late at night the rain comes down so heavily that nobody can leave,[1] and Pandarus puts Criseyde up in a little room. He then comes to tell her that Troilus (who has been in the house all the time), has just arrived in agony at a rumour that she has given her love to one Horaste. Thus Criseyde is led to comfort Troilus, and to protest her innocence. As she does so, and weeps at the thought of the insinuations, Troilus is so smitten with grief and remorse that he does the only free action he has performed yet: he swoons. This puts Criseyde, pushed on by Pandarus, in the role of comforter, and from there to physical involvement is little distance: but even then Pandarus is still there to take the candle away and make sure that they are certain to consummate their love before leaving them to it.

To a lesser extent, Pandarus is still involved in manipulating Troilus in Books IV and V. He pulls Troilus far enough out of his despair to go and talk matters over with Criseyde (IV.616–58). In Book V he is still managing Troilus' feelings, keeping him 'up to the mark' and taking him to Sarpedon's palace; and, despite his own doubts, he keeps Troilus' hopes stoked, even getting him to write a letter to Criseyde when he fails to think of doing it for himself (1296 ff.). It is not surprising therefore that Troilus should debate the issue of free will versus necessity (IV.953–1078): he himself has given up free will long previously.

It is true that, had Troilus and Criseyde been more active in forwarding their relationship, and more involved with making arrangements for their meetings, we might feel their love to be less refined and intense. Certainly Boccaccio's Criseida, who is more 'busy' and available than Criseyde, is worldly and less attractive, and the passion between her and Troilo more narrowly physical.[2] Criseida is faithless because, Boccaccio tells us, all young

[1] The rain itself is not destinal as W. C. Curry, *Chaucer and the Medieval Sciences* (2nd ed., New York, 1960), pp. 260–1, claims: Pandarus has foreseen it and arranged for Criseyde to be in his house when it comes; his foresight could not simply be to the lighter rain in which he persuades her to come from her house to his, or else she could as easily have returned. And of course, despite her remaining at Pandarus' house, Criseyde still has it in her power to refuse Troilus. See also Kean, 137–41.

[2] On this see e.g. Kean, pp. 114–15, 117–18.

women are fickle:[1] Chaucer's Criseyde fails through the very nature of the love to which she and Troilus give themselves. Troilus refuses to impose himself on her in any way and therefore does not possess her. Both she and Troilus voluntarily surrender their free wills, abandon engagement with the world and turn love into an absolute: but while by thus enclosing and isolating their love they make their relationship come to a white heat of purity and intensity, they at the same time make it and themselves absolutely open to vicissitude. To experience the highest joys of human love, Chaucer seems to be saying, you must put yourself in a potentially tragic and at least formally sinful position of total disengagement from the world, in a perverted asceticism.

Elements other than Troilus' disengagement from society and patriotic motivation, and his and Criseyde's passivity, bring home the isolation of the lovers. Of these the first is secrecy. But for their concealment of their love the exchange of Criseyde for Antenor might never have taken place, since the Trojans would have been unwilling to upset the happiness of one of their finest warriors and leaders. By the courtly love code one central element which necessitated secrecy was here missing: Criseyde was not a wife but a widow, and the love is not adulterous. But Andreas Capellanus also mentions that secrecy is necessary to preserve the integrity of love, not only from the gossip of calumniators (a very real factor for Criseyde), but also to keep the love from leaking away in public knowledge;[2] and whether or not Chaucer is following Andreas or any of his imitators, we feel very strongly in this poem that the intensity of the love is founded on its concealment, on the idea of infinite riches in a little room of knowledge.

On both of the first occasions when Troilus and Criseyde meet, we are aware of a public world which has been duped and shut out for the purpose. Nor is that world portrayed as corrupt: Troilus' brothers and Helen are eager to help Criseyde in her sup-

---

[1] *Filostrato*, VIII. st. 28.

[2] See John J. Parry, *The Art of Courtly Love of Andreas Capellanus*, Columbia University Records of Civilization: Sources and Studies, No. 33 (New York Univ. Press, 1941), p. 81, Rule VI; p. 185, Rule XIII; and pp. 175, 177.

posed plight with Poliphete, and we feel a sense of dismay that Pandarus has awakened such charity in the public world only to deceive it; one wonders too, if more faintly, what became of the falsely accused Poliphete. Here, too, we are jarred when Troilus secures the departure of the solicitous Deiphebus and Helen from his supposed sickroom by handing them a paper of Hector's to peruse, concerning the possible execution of a man (II.1692–1701);[1] on their return we are told how Troilus 'gan ful lightly of the lettre pace' (III.220).[2] Both the meetings of the lovers, in Deiphebus' and in Pandarus' house, take place in little rooms: we perhaps have a sense that the inner sanctum of love is being reached, or that the love is best realized thus surrounded and enclosed by a world that knows nothing of it, but we must also feel the sense that it is claustrophobic, enclosed, hothouse (the word 'stewe' for 'little room' had also the meaning 'brothel').

In this connection another factor must be the curses of night and of day (developed from brief mentions in Boccaccio) uttered by the lovers when they must part after their nights of pleasure in Pandarus' house:

'Thow doost, allas, to shortly thyn office,
Thow rakle nyght, ther God, maker of kynde,
The, for thyn haste and thyn unkynde vice,
So faste ey to oure hemysperie bynde,
That nevere more under the ground thow wynde!' (III.1436–40)

'O cruel day, accusour of the joie
That nyght and love han stole and faste iwryen,
Acorsed be thi comyng into Troye . . . .' (III.1450–2)

---

[1] It is surely mistaken to claim, as Kean p. 148 does, that the background of such excellent figures of Trojan society as Hector or Helen casts favourable light on Troilus and Criseyde, in a context where Troilus is duping them.

[2] And Troilus is elsewhere quite ready to put his love before anyone else when he offers Pandarus his sisters Polyxena or Cassandra, and even Helen herself, as recompense for his services (III.409–13). It is true that this is a largely impractical idea, and one resulting from an overflow of excitement (Troilus becomes quite indiscriminate with his '"or any of the frape"'); and that it is inaccurate to see this as simply reprehensible (Robertson, pp. 489–90, Kean, p. 128): yet the basic attitude revealed is exposed to criticism.

And day they gonnen to despise al newe,
Callyng it traitour, envyous, and worse,
And bitterly the dayes light thei corse. (III.1699–1701)[1]

Troilus goes on to refuse to do further sacrifice to the sun. In these curses of both night and day Chaucer has portrayed a rejection of all time. At this point the love of Troilus and Criseyde has set itself against every other value, and above the subjection of mutable things to the categories both of time and place.

It is this that makes the love most open to subjection by these categories: for when the lovers cut themselves off from the world, they render themselves unable to control its alterations. They remain finally will-less and inert, and this guarantees their tragedy. When Troilus first hears of the projected exchange of Antenor for Criseyde, he immediately despairs utterly:

'What shal I don? I shal, while I may dure
On lyve in torment and in cruwel peyne,
This infortune or this disaventure,
Allone as I was born, iwys, compleyne;
Ne nevere wol I seen it shyne or reyne,
But ende I wol, as Edippe, in derknesse
My sorwful lif, and dyen in distresse.' (IV.295–301)

He goes on to picture future lovers passing by his sepulchre (323–9). There is a hint of self-dramatization about Troilus: he seems to want to see himself as the man hard done by, as a type of the great but unfortunate lover; perhaps, at bottom, his passivity is a function not only of the nature of the love to which he gives himself, but also of a wish for the very doom he experiences.[2] At any rate, from now on he frequently looks to the ultimate of passivity, his own death.

[1] There are very close analogies here with lines in Donne's 'The Sunne Rising', though Donne belittles the sun where Troilus, acknowledging its power, can only revile it. See particularly l.1454, '"what list the so to spien?"' and ll.1461–2, '"What profrestow thi light here for to selle?/Go selle it hem that smale selys grave."' It may be, however, that both poets had a common source in Ovid, *Amores*, I.xiii.

[2] Theodore A. Stroud, 'Boethius' Influence on Chaucer's Troilus', *MP*, XLIX (1951–2), 5, remarks in Troilus 'a passivity, a craving for failure, hardly typical of the courtly lover, much less of romance in general'.

Pandarus, of course, who now enters, has other ideas. He proposes the detachment of which Troilus is incapable, suggesting
that Troilus has had a good time with Criseyde already, that she is
not the only pebble on the beach, that it is mere '"nyce vanitee"'
not to take the woman one loves, and that gossip soon dies down
(IV.393–427, 526–39, 582–630, 1093–1120). Troilus replies in under-
standable outrage to the first suggestions; for the others, he argues
that with the exchange confirmed by his father Priam in parliament, the public weal will not be turned aside for private feli-
city,[1] and that any attempt to take Criseyde with him from Troy
would produce a slander on her name which he could not allow.
Moral principle is thus opposed to realism: but the ultimate
polarity is between passivity and activity. Though Troilus is
finally persuaded to discuss leaving Troy with Criseyde if she
agrees with the idea (which Pandarus then goes to her to find out),
he relapses into fatalism in Pandarus' absence, giving vent to his
long soliloquy on free will and determinism (IV.953–1078), in
which he concludes that '"al that comth, comth by necessitee"'
(958). On his return Pandarus has to labour once more to bring
Troilus to move. He bids him consider that he knows nothing of
what is in Criseyde's mind, and that he, Pandarus, has been with
her and senses that she has a scheme to put to Troilus (1100–13);
at which Troilus gloomily agrees to go and see her.

Meanwhile Criseyde herself has been bewailing the news, and
accepting that separation from Troilus is final separation and her
death (731–91); though, unlike Troilus, what wounds her more
than her own misery is the thought of the sorrow she will cause
Troilus (794–5, 855–61, 897–908). Pandarus, who for more
worldly reasons has begun to accept that the love may be lost,
now enters and bids her put on a good face for Troilus, who is
coming to see her, '"Beth rather to hym cause of flat than egge"'
(927). He warns her that Troilus will put forward schemes for
saving the situation, and tells her to cheer him up by encouraging

---

[1] He also argues (547–50) that since Troy was first brought to war by the rape
of Helen, people will reprehend any further ravishment. To this idealist position Pandarus poses the equally valid worldly alternative of following the example of Paris: '"Thenk ek how Paris hath, that is thi brother,/A love; and whi
shaltow nat have another?"' (608–9).

him in this, whether in the idea of her fleeing with him from Troy or in that of her coming back to him in Troy from the Greek camp (885–96, 925–38). Criseyde's meeting with Troilus is thus planned less as a discussion of practical remedies than as a discussion of such remedies in order that Troilus' spirits may be lifted: it is a function of this that Criseyde speaks only of the action which she might perform later, namely, her return to Troy from the Greek camp. It would be wrong, of course, to see Criseyde simply as holding Troilus in hand: she herself is partially cheered up by her own schemes and projects even while in herself she feels them impossible. Thus it is that when Troilus arrives she goes into considerable detail over how the Greek camp is but a small distance from Troy, so that she can easily return, and will do so within ten days, which, she points out, is a smaller length of time than that which often separates the lovers in Troy (1310–30); and she argues that her father may want her back through groundless suspicion that she is being badly treated in Troy for his defection (1338–44). She continues by outlining how hearsay has it that peace, and therefore easy commerce between Trojans and Greeks, is near: this of course is to go back on her declaration to return to Troy, to which she now quickly reverts (1359–65). Then she offers—'"Have here another wey, if it so be/That al this thyng ne may yow nat suffise"' (1366–7)—the much more obviously desperate female ploy of cheating her covetous father with the promise of her wealth in Troy, which he will return her to secure; and she even proposes convincing him that the gods which seemed to tell him Troy would fall were misinterpreted (1368–1414).

Troilus is less than happy, particularly at the naked impracticality of her proposals regarding Calchas, which casts uncertainty on all her projects (1450–6). He voices his dread lest Criseyde be tempted by the attractions of the Greek men, and argues for her fleeing with him from Troy (1471–1526). She swears by her truth to him and refuses his plan on the grounds that it would dishonour them both and would be a treachery to Troy from which Troilus could never clear himself, and for which she would be responsible (1534–82). She concludes, first, with an insistence on accepting the inevitable, an inevitability which Troilus has already in his long soliloquy admitted to govern the world—'"Thus maketh vertu of necessite/By patience"' (1586-7); and then, inconsistent with this philosophy, repeats her intention of returning to Troy before the tenth day from her departure (1583-1638).

We are aware throughout all this that it is the finest of human motives, namely, love and respect for the honour of the other person—Troilus' prestige in Troy, Criseyde's good name—that is the efficient cause of the lovers' passivity before events; aware too that Pandarus' suggestion of other possibilities is in a sense vulgar. But we have also observed the passivity of the lovers throughout their affair, and in Book IV we have seen both of them announce themselves determinists—Troilus in his long speech on predestination, Criseyde in her private reaction to the news of the exchange and in her desire more to cheer up Troilus and herself than to act. Moreover, the very advancing of plans by which they might remedy their plight only to dismiss them heightens the disconnection of the lovers from the world and from action. And the bitter irony is that all the nobility and honour deployed in the lovers' refusal to go against the good of Troy and Priam's public decree are ultimately wasted, since Antenor is to turn traitor to Troy. It would have been better for the town had Troilus refused to relinquish Criseyde: the superior perception of national value which, in their isolation, the lovers allow Priam and his parliament is not to be demonstrated.

In Book V the love of Troilus and Criseyde, which they severed from the outer world, becomes subject to it, and to time and place. Criseyde goes to the Greek camp and contemplates Troilus in Troy; and has ten days in which to return to him. Likewise the predicament of Troilus in Troy: he counts the days and becomes increasingly aware of the location of his previous relationship with Criseyde. The war of two societies now rolls between, and each of the lovers is now reduced to seeing the other as caught up in a larger public body.

The passive acceptance by the lovers that they must part has accomplished most of the tragic action: what follows does so almost inevitably from the new conditions. Separated from the world of public events as they have become, the lovers lack the will or the ability to manage the world in their own interests. Troilus toys momentarily with the idea of entering the Greek camp in disguise, but drops it (v.1576–82); and he has been so concerned with Criseyde as his love rather than as a woman that he has not really given full consideration to the obstacles to one of her character in attempting to steal away through a vigilant army. Both of the lovers are unable to plan ahead realistically, or as Criseyde puts it, '"future tyme, er I was in the snare,/Koude I nat sen"' (v.748–9). It is true that in not entering into a definite and practical scheme they are showing their faith in one another; and true that there is an element of noble submission in the way they bow to their separation: yet nevertheless our main impression is of a fatal isolation from the world, and a consequent paralysis of will.

Once in the Greek camp, all Criseyde's naïve projects collapse: Calchas is obdurate, the Greeks vigilant, peace is remote, Troy may be doomed and truth in love is less certain than she thought. She had vaguely imagined that she might use Calchas' desires to accomplish her own: but without the former, she is reduced to need for an effort of personal will to return to Troy from which she shrinks. Chaucer, of course, is sympathetic: it is hard for woman, who has a more passive nature than man in any case, to be put in a plight like this. Yet the moral analysis is also as clear as it is in *The Legend of Good Women*, in the portraits of Cleopatra or Thisbe and their courageous assertions of faith and love in their deaths.

The behaviour of Diomede highlights the passivity both of Criseyde and of Troilus. Diomede, unlike Troilus, is 'active': needing no intermediary, he himself pushes his attentions on Criseyde in a kind of emotional rape. She is bewildered by 'this sodeyn Diomede' (v.1024),[1] and we are to believe that he succeeds by forcefully imposing himself on her passive nature.

[1] Lawlor, p. 60, points out the earlier example of her bewilderment at the 'sodeyn', when Troilus is brought to her in Pandarus' house: 'Ne though men sholde smyten of hire hed,/She kouthe nought a word aright out-brynge/So sodeynly, for his sodeyn comynge' (III.957–9).

Troilus was never dominant or active in his relationship with her: indeed it is she who finds herself seducing him, and she too puts down all his suggestions and forbids all his doubts before she quits Troy. Of course Troilus' behaviour stemmed partly from his sense of honour, his refusal to violate the wishes of his lady: but as well as seeing this as one of the highest values in love, we are also aware that it may be taken as an excess of fastidiousness, and that Troilus and Diomede represent the two aspects of masculine love which should be joined, but are divided and at war, as are Greeks and Trojans. Diomede's courtship is described in terms of a siege, and we feel that his love is an extension of his warrior-role, where that of Troilus is not: in this sense Diomede, while he is certainly no ideal, joins the public and private worlds in his behaviour. To the extent that Diomede imposes himself on Criseyde where Troilus did not, he is likely to succeed, if what he gains is a love of less value: and to this same extent Criseyde's passivity is to be attributed to that of Troilus. And in the larger scheme of the war, of which we are now much more conscious, Troy, of which Troilus is a part, is the passive, the besieged and the doomed, where the Greeks are the active, the victors-to-be: on this wider level therefore, expressed in the actions and natures of the charac-ters, Diomede's defeat of Troilus is inevitable. Just before Troilus finally discovers Criseyde's infidelity, the narrator describes the destruction of Hector, and therein the beginning of that of Troy (v.1548–65): the process portrayed—'Fortune . . ./Gan pulle awey the fetheres brighte of Troie/Fro day to day, til they ben bare of joie' (v.1541, 1546–7)—takes that of Troilus into the larger pattern. But neither Troilus' passivity compared to Dio-mede, nor the wider context of history serves to cancel Criseyde's failure of will, her lack of resistance to obstreperous circumstance: for that we must return to the fundamental dissociation from the world of the love which she and Troilus shared. She has been brought to see Troy and Troilus in relative terms: she has be-come aware of a wider world and of another place, a place from which Troy itself is seen as but one place; and, letting this take over her mind, her values too become finally relative—'"al shal passe; and thus take I my leve"' (v.1085). When time and place become the measure of her love; when she must go from the Greek camp to Troilus in Troy within ten days: then her love becomes conditioned by time and place, worn down by days, distance and Diomede.

The burden of faith is not upon Troilus, and his love does not alter:[1] when he knows of Criseyde's faithlessness he still declares, "'I ne can nor may,/For all this world, withinne myn herte fynde/To unloven yow a quarter of a day!'" (v.1696–8). But if Troilus' love does not change, his hope, his trust and his attachment to life itself are shown under the eroding influence of time and space throughout Book v. On the seventh day after Criseyde's departure he can bear no longer the diversions of Sarpedon's house, and hurries home in hope of finding that Criseyde has returned to her palace in his absence: his wretchedness at the bleak emptiness of her house is portrayed in detail (v.528–60). Now that Criseyde has gone, he has only the shells of space that once held her, spaces he could ignore when she was with him, "'O paleys empty and disconsolat,/O thow lanterne of which queynt is the light,/ .../O ryng, fro which the ruby is out falle'" (542–3, 549). He tours the sites of his amorous experiences (561–81), as if to call up his love by association, but the scenes awaken only pain (582–95); and he goes to the gates of Troy where he relinquished Criseyde, to relive the fact of his separation and suffering (603–16). Everything is now conditioned by place. And there is no emotional certainty: the pains will be cancelled by Criseyde's return, and the joys of hope and trust lost should she fail, but in the meantime Troilus must hang between the two. The portrayal after this is one of a continual reaching for and falling away from certainty, in the repeated fixing and postponement of time. Criseyde had vowed to return *by* the tenth day, but gradually both she and Troilus make it the day of return. When Criseyde does not come during the tenth day, Troilus argues that Calchas has detained her and that she will be there by evening; when

---

[1] Indeed the rigidity of Troilus and his love is set almost dialectically against the fluidity of Criseyde; a picture perhaps expanded by Shakespeare in his conception of the inflexible idealist who refuses to admit or adjust to the alterations of the mutable world, whether in Helen or Cressida.

evening is gone he considers that she has sensibly decided to steal ever by night; and when the next day has come he eventually falls back on Criseyde's declaration that she would come when the moon had passed out of Leo, that is, on the eleventh day (1100–90).[1] The eleventh day gone, Troilus retains some hope until the sixth day beyond the tenth, after which he gives himself to despair (1205–11). Now a new source of uncertainty, the suspicion that Criseyde may have betrayed him, is awakened in him and quickened by his dream of Criseyde in the 'arms' of a boar. Pandarus is able to contrive an innocuous interpretation of this dream, but Troilus requires certainty, and on Pandarus' encouragement writes to Criseyde asking her why she has delayed. The answer gives some renewed expectation of her return, but Troilus' hopes are not now raised far, and are soon worn down again (1436–42); and some of the comfort Pandarus' interpretation of his dream lent him is removed by the more expert diagnosis of Cassandra (1450–1535). Again Troilus writes to Criseyde, and again there is uncertain assurance of return (1583–1638). Troilus at last reaches truth and certainty when he discovers the brooch he gave to Criseyde on the captured armour of Diomede (1646–1701). At this point he determines to leave the uncertain and mutable world of place and time altogether, by seeking his own death.

The seasonal imagery of Books IV and V is wintry,[2] and quite apart from the waiting for Criseyde's return there is a stress on the indifferent movement of time which is not present in the first three books;[3] and from the beginning of Book IV we are made aware of the larger context of the war irrespective of Troilus' doings in it. What we have throughout these books is a picture of wider change in which the lovers are swept up. Till now they

---

[1] Meanwhile, of course, Criseyde, the cause of these postponements, is shown fixing and falling away from the deadline of the tenth day also: '"withouten any wordes mo,/To Troie I wole, as for conclusioun"' (764–5). Chaucer underlines the irony: 'God it wot, er fully monthes two,/She was ful fer fro that entencioun!'

[2] See Henry W. Sams, 'The Dual Time-Scheme in Chaucer's *Troilus*', *MLN*, LVI (1941), 98–100.

[3] See e.g. IV.43–9; V.8–14, 267–73, 1016–22. Where time was mentioned before, it was as the measure of love's growth.

have imposed their desires and private values on time, space and the public world, but now time and space impose themselves on them, mocking them with partings, distant city walls, empty palaces, long hours of complaint and waiting, and broken appointments. The world they cut themselves off from, the war they largely forgot and the dreary succession of night and day they cursed return in power; and, passive and disengaged as the lovers are, they can do nothing to prevent indifferent circumstance doing what it will with them until, in their separate ways, what they were is worn away. In the midst of the action of the final book, Chaucer suddenly follows a sketch of Diomede with two pictures (not in Boccaccio) of Criseyde and Troilus (806–40) which, by their very 'fixing' of physical appearance and character serve further to bring home the note of mutability and transience: we get an impression of distance, like looking at old photographs, and the effect is one of being introduced, as if we had not known them before.

> Criseyde mene was of hire stature,
> Therto of shap, of face and ek of cheere,
> Ther myghte ben no fairer creature.
> And ofte tyme this was hire manere,
> To gon ytressed with hire heres clere
> Doun by hire coler at hire bak byhynde,
> Which with a thred of gold she wolde bynde.
>
> And, save hire browes joyneden yfere,
> There nas no lak, in aught I kan espien . . . .
>
> She sobre was, ek symple, and wys withal,
> The best ynorisshed ek that myghte be,
> And goodly of hire speche in general,
> Charitable, estatlich, lusty, and fre;
> Ne nevere mo ne lakked hire pite;
> Tendre-herted, slydynge of corage;
> But trewely, I kan nat telle hire age.

The picture of Troilus deals similarly with physical appearance and character traits: and indeed, if we look back, we find that we have been told little of these hitherto;[1] by so fully stating them here, Chaucer is establishing the lovers as individual people of flesh and blood, and in so doing is making us additionally conscious of the frailty of that individuality. The very definition of shape and character in this context makes them tremble on the edge of dissolution.

At the end, burdened by the fact that he cannot cease loving Criseyde, that he cannot detach himself from his love, Troilus resolves to seek his death, to use the war as a way of ending himself. But the detachment he gains after his death is as unbalanced as the previous amorous involvement: then he was too far inside love, now he is too far out of it. His tone of wounded spite as he surveys the world from the Olympian vantage point of the eighth sphere of the heavens to which he ascends underlines the inadequacy of his strictures:

> And down from thennes faste he gan avyse
> This litel spot of erthe, that with the se
> Embraced is, and fully gan despise
> This wrecched world, and held al vanite
> To respect of the pleyn felicite
> That is in hevene above; and at the laste,
> Ther he was slayn, his lokyng down he caste.
>
> And in hymself he lough right at the wo
> Of hem that wepten for his deth so faste;
> And dampned al oure werk that foloweth so
> The blynde lust, the which that may nat laste,
> And sholden al oure herte on heven caste. (v.1814–25)

Here of course the detachment is total, being not simply from his personal relationship but from the whole world: but the world is an extension of the love experience, wherein no mortal joy is sure; the whole earth becomes the private and 'involved' world of the sublunar quest for happiness, conducted in neglect of the wider 'public' obligations of heaven. To be sure, Troilus' strictures offer

---

[1] As John Bayley puts it, 'we are quite separated now from the consciousness of love that ignores external appearances' (*The Characters of Love* (1960), p. 121.)

a point of view, and the narrator goes on to extend and Christianize them as he ends the poem. Further, the strictures are at least partly borne out from within the poem in the implicit statement behind such blasphemies[1] as Pandarus' '"Immortal god . . . that mayst nought deyen,/Cupid I mene"' (III.185–6); the narrator's comment on Criseyde's reaction to Pandarus' machinations, 'What! God foryaf his deth, and she al so/Foryaf' (III.1577–8);[2] or the constant references to love in religious terminology of grace, mercy and desert, and to love's foundation in Venus rather than God.[3] But the narrator has either agreed—passively[4]—with whatever the lovers do, or else refused to condemn them throughout the poem, and the same narrator utters the hymn to Venus at the beginning of Book III: he himself has been heavily 'involved' in the love, and he himself is attempting the distressed lurch into detachment that Troilus makes at the end.[5] Such detachment is as inadequate as blind involvement: one must try to unite the two;[6] there should be, in the words of George Eliot's dictum,

[1] The word 'blasphemy' is applicable here in direct and indirect senses. That of the narrator, who lives in medieval and Christian times, is direct blasphemy; and that of the characters in the poem, though they lived before Christianity, does indirectly reflect upon them by heightening their benightedness.

[2] See also e.g. I.1002–8; II.894–6; more glaring perhaps is the image used by Pandarus to remove Criseyde's fears of gossip should Troilus visit her, '"What? who wol demen, though he se a man/To temple go, that he th'ymages eteth?"' (II.372–3), or the irony of Criseyde's oath, '"What, par dieux! I am naught religious"' (II.759). For contexts in which 'God', the 'love of God' or 'heaven' are invoked, with double reference for the reader, see e.g. II.500; III.951, 1251, 1289–92, 1656–9, 1744–71. And Troilus divinizes Criseyde (I.102–05, 425–7 and IV.450–1; though tempered by Pandarus at I.981–4).

[3] See e.g. I.895–6; II.1524–6; III.1254–74.

[4] This word is also, of course, relevant to the narrator's frequent portrayal of himself as helpless before the facts of the story (e.g. I.1–14; II.8–18, 49; IV.12–21; 1037–50, 1093–9, 1772–8). See also Morton W. Bloomfield, 'Distance and Predestination in *Troilus and Criseyde*', *PMLA*, LXXII (1957), 18–24.

[5] See also Lawlor, pp. 67–9. Lawlor also comments on the narrator's language, 'the energy of protest and assertion is its own testimony to the disturbance he has undergone' (p. 68). The same could be said of the bitter, spiteful tone of Troilus; and it is surely this, as much as the matter of *what* is said that has made many commentators uneasy at the close of the poem; it is not sufficient to try to reconcile only the bare philosophy expressed here with the rest of the poem.

[6] For a fine attempt to show how both may be joined in a compassionate irony underlying the whole poem, see Gordon, passim.

'no private life that is not determined by a wider public life'[1] as much as vice versa. And Chaucer himself lies both further in and further out than the limited visions with which the characters of his poem begin and end: he teaches us dialectically.

'For may no man fordon the lawe of kynde': Chaucer knows that love, which binds creation, can be as potent and hard to resist as Troilus finds it. He also probably knew that 'The irresistibility of love, love as the sole source of human worth, the moral code of Courtly Love based on these two principles, were formally condemned on March 7, 1277, by Archbishop Stephen Tempier at Paris as manifest and execrable errors.'[2] In *The Parliament of Fowls*, after reading Africanus' world-renouncing injunctions to Scipio, the narrator is left in some discontent: 'For bothe I hadde thyng which that I nolde,/ And ek I nadde that thyng that I wolde' (90-1). For Chaucer, to the phenomenon of love and its effects no simple rejectionist answer is adequate. Equally, however, wholesale absorption of the self in love is both selfish and wrong. The dilemma has been well summed up in Eliot's 'Teach us to care and not to care.'[3] There can be no clear prescriptive answer at all as to the nature and management of this balance.[4] All Chaucer shows us is that if love is pursued as a final value, to the exclusion of all other modes of awareness, earthly and heavenly, it is at once exceptionally rich and intense, and open to destruction.

The double perspective extends to the religious and secular modes of possible detachment. If Chaucer had wanted to write a simply 'Boethian' poem, in which the only answer was to ground one's life on heaven, he would have done better to create a situation—say, a natural calamity, sudden death or mortal illness—in which the disaster could not be averted by practical means: for

[1] *Felix Holt*, ch. III.

[2] Alexander J. Denomy, C.S.B., 'The Two Moralities of Chaucer's *Troilus and Criseyde*', *Transactions of the Royal Society of Canada*, XLIV, Ser. III, sec. 2 (June, 1950), repr. in R. J. Schoeck and J. Taylor, eds., *Chaucer Criticism II: 'Troilus and Criseyde' and The Minor Poems* (Notre Dame, Indiana, 1961), p. 153. See also p. 155, and Boethius, *De Consolatione*, III, Met. 12, 52–70.

[3] Also cited in this connection by James L. Shanley, 'The *Troilus* and Christian Love', *ELH*, VI (1939), 279.

[4] Though James I of Scotland, in his *The Kingis Quair* (?1424), later attempts one.

then the only consolation would be *contemptus mundi*, as it was for the plight of Boethius. But he has given us a story in which the unfortunate situation could have been manipulated by the lovers to their advantage. In a context where fortune may be defeated by worldly and practical means the doctrine that the only surety against earthly vicissitude is to be found in religion is relegated to the position of a second, if infallible, line of defence. It is true that, through a glass darkly, the severance of Chaucer's lovers from the outside world can be seen as a figure of their severance from the heavenly world also.[1] But it is clear that the religious answer is only the ultimate, and not the sole solution offered to the tragedy of Troilus and Criseyde.

[1] Rather more, certainly, than the world-renunciation of Troilus and Criseyde, founded on earthly love, figures that asked of Boethius by Philosophy.

II

Shakespeare and Milton

RACHEL TRICKETT

'The effect of masterpieces on me is to make me admire and do otherwise,' wrote Gerard Manley Hopkins, an observation characteristic at once of his originality and his limitations. Less self-conscious poets lack this sense of rivalry, and minor writers have always relied on imitation as their guarantee of survival. But masters, if not masterpieces, affected even Hopkins. The early Keatsianism of *A Vision of Mermaids* surfaces in a vivid recollection in *The Wreck of the Deutschland*, where Joy's grape of the *Ode to Melancholy* reappears as a 'lush-kept, plush-capped sloe' which

> will, mouthed to flesh-burst
> Gush!—flush the man, the being with it, sour or sweet,
> Brim, in a flash, full!

This is a remarkable elaboration of Keats's image if not entirely a successful one. In Hopkins's sloe, mumbled in the mouth, we miss the clear action of the original, the 'strenuous tongue', and the end of his sentence is such an instance of almost Jamesian syntactical affectation that it disturbs the enthusiastic tone. Keats's sensuousness is here; his sincerity seems lacking. A poet like Hopkins whose consciousness of his own skills and needs drove him to forge a style in defiance of past-masters, when he alludes to them produces a boldly obvious, almost a competitive imitation.

There are roughly two kinds of imitation in good poetry: this obvious sort, of a whole range from allusion to parody which is consciously employed and meant to be recognized, and a kind that is only semi-conscious on the poet's part, and may be hard to detect in detail though apparent in the overall tone of a work, or vice-versa. But within these two categories there are innumerable

varieties to satisfy source-hunters and encourage critical speculation. I propose to deal here with some examples of the influence
on Milton of Shakespeare for a particular purpose—not as an
instance of simple literary imitation, but to illustrate an aspect of
the way in which the poetic imagination works.

One of the fallacies we fall into most readily is to assume that
poets read poetry as critics do. This is seldom the case. Poets are
rarely systematic, and their reading is almost always positive. On
the whole, few great poets (Pope and Blake being possible excep-
tions) have been underestimated by their peers. The reason for
this is the respect of one craftsman for another. For poets the art of
writing comes first, and they read another's work not for his
ideas on life but for his mastery of technique, his peculiar craft. In
doing so they seldom fail to acknowledge a member of the fraternity even if his vision might seem to us to conflict with theirs.
Dryden loved Chaucer and caught something of his narrative
art; Pope imitated wholesale though he tried to cover up the
traces of minor poets' influence; Byron reverted to Pope; Wordsworth admired Dryden's *Fables* (the most imitative of his poems);
Keats copied Spenser, Shakespeare, Milton and Dryden almost
indiscriminately. Even poet-critics like Eliot when they are
absorbed in their art leave on one side the prescriptive judgments
they make in their prose. The Romantics are slighted in Eliot's
criticism, but the presence of Shelley and Wordsworth is unmis-
takeable in his verse plays and in *Four Quartets*. According to
Aubrey, Dryden said that Milton acknowledged to him that
Spenser was his original. Careful reading shows that Shakespeare
infiltrated his poetry as often and no less significantly.

In her article, '*Comus* and Shakespeare', printed in *Essays and
Studies*, Vol. XXXI, 1945, Ethel Seaton first traced the extraordi-
narily close verbal echoes in Milton's masque of *Romeo and Juliet*, *A
Midsummer Night's Dream* and *The Tempest*. Her work leaves the
reader in no doubt as to the intimate engagement of Milton's
imagination at this stage with Shakespeare, especially with his
lyrical plays. Previous critics who had cited the influence of
Spenser, John Fletcher and Ben Jonson on the form and theme of
the masque, had not noticed its pervasive Shakespearian mood,

and ignored what Dr Seaton so closely pursued—the many verbal reminiscences of works that had penetrated even below the consciousness which is so marked an element in Milton's art.

At first sight, and bearing in mind Keats's distinction between their two types of genius, it might seem that no one was less likely to touch Milton's imagination than Shakespeare. The twentieth-century attack on Milton was precisely on account of his lack of Shakespearian concreteness and immediacy. Even the celebratory lines on Shakespeare, Milton's first published verses which were appended to the Second Folio of 1632, could be read as a formal and conceited encomium rather than a spontaneous appreciation. But a disinterested reading of Milton shows a remarkable grasp on his part of Shakespeare's imaginative vision, distinct though it is from his own, and Dr Seaton's article stands as a unique early recognition of this. In his annotations to *Paradise Lost* A. W. Verity records a number of Shakespearian allusions, but draws no inferences from them—understandably perhaps, since the epic exhibits less deep indebtedness to Shakespeare than Milton's minor poems. Dr Seaton's modest but original contention that the argument for chastity in *Comus* is related to the celebration of natural love in *Romeo and Juliet* is not merely important for the sake of argument; it reveals the play of the poetic imagination on issues which, at first sight and to reason, might seem incompatible.

In the holograph annotations to her copy of the facsimile of the Trinity College manuscripts of Milton's minor poems, Ethel Seaton pursued her investigations of Milton's memory of Shakespeare. One of the most curious—recorded later by Helen Darbishire and Professor Carey in the Oxford and Longman editions respectively—is a reference to *Pericles* in the Trinity College manuscript version of *Lycidas*. Milton wrote there at line 157, 'Where thou perhaps under the *humming* tide', an epithet later emended to 'whelming'. The peculiar adjective recalls Pericles' lament over Thaisa in III.i.64–6:

> the belching whale
> And humming water must o'erwhelm thy corpse,
> Lying with simple shells.

Milton's encomium on Shakespeare had been composed in 1630 before the publication of the Second Folio, and he could not have read *Pericles* in either the First or Second Folios, as it was only included in the corpus in the second impression of the Third printed in 1663. There cannot have been many of his learned contemporaries who cared enough for Shakespeare to follow him in the Quartos as well as in the Folio which established his literary fame, but Milton's acquaintance with *Pericles* must have come from these. It is a striking instance of his admiration and his imaginative response that, in writing his elegy in 1637 his thoughts turned to Pericles' speech which he must have read in the Quarto reprints of 1630 or 1635 (it was from the last of these that the Third Folio text of the play was taken).

To modern editors (as to Milton) the speech is undoubtedly Shakespeare's:

> A terrible childbed hast thou had, my dear,
> No light, no fire: th'unfriendly elements
> Forgot thee utterly; nor have I time
> To give thee hallow'd to thy grave, but straight
> Must cast thee, scarcely coffin'd, in the ooze;
> Where, for a monument upon thy bones,
> And e'er-remaining lamps, the belching whale
> And humming water must o'erwhelm thy corpse,
> Lying with simple shells.
>
>   (III.i.55–64)

The simple shells, and the understated poignancy of the first line seem particularly Shakespearian now. *Lycidas* is a supreme effort of artifice in which nothing is or appears to be understated, but the unfriendly elements are an essential part of the questioning of the poem from its opening. Shakespeare's lines are strikingly appropriate as a counterpart to Milton's feelings. We cannot suppose deliberate allusion since few seventeenth-century readers are likely to have known the play.[1] Milton may well have changed 'humming' to 'whelming' to avoid for himself any obvious reminiscence, though the final word clearly came from the same

[1] *Pericles* was, however, a very popular performing play until the closing of the theatres.

obstinate source. It is impossible to judge how consciously words echo in a poet's memory. But though we cannot affirm that Milton was openly recalling Shakespeare here, we must see that his imagination was deeply engaged with the similar experiences behind his poem and Shakespeare's play. It tells us something about the nature of *Lycidas* as a poem to recognize this. The elegy lacks light and fire—for it concentrates on the elements of earth and water and only in the apotheosis does the day-star that 'with new-spangled ore/Flames in the forehead of the morning sky' introduce ideas of comfort and illumination. But the violence of the drowning, the sea tearing apart Lycidas's bones, emphasizes the terror of the unfriendly elements and the youth they forgot utterly. Milton does not try to conceal the harshness of the universe that lies behind the pastoral artifice of the poem.

The Shakespearian influences that permeated *Comus* are still present in *Lycidas*, written two years later. The sea in the poem, a powerful presence, is never wholly an agent of destruction. Equally in Shakespeare's romances it is an agent of restoration—giving up its dead to be reanimated after storm and shipwreck.

The watery paradise of *Lycidas* with its echoes of the sea of Galilee where Christ walked the waves, and the pure nectar of Elysium, can only be conceived of after the turn of the tide which concludes Milton's lament on the cruelty of death. That he was thinking of Shakespeare at this point is as important as that he should have boldly united Christian and pagan myth, recalled to learned readers Sannazaro's piscatory eclogues, and used the common symbolic associations of water as the element of baptism and renewal as well as of grief. All these are well-known and often-noted scholarly connections, but they do not tell us as much about what Milton felt here as the fact that his imagination instinctively turned to *Pericles*.

The traffic is two-way: we can understand something more in Shakespeare's romances as well, if we see how another great poet read them. In this new light the later plays appear, in some sense, elegiac. Not from the tiredness Lytton Strachey attributed to them, but in the way they play with the basic themes of pastoral elegy—catastrophe, questioning, resolution. Each of the plays,

Pericles, The Winter's Tale and *The Tempest*, has a harsh and violent tragedy to present or recount in its first part; each resolves the dilemma irrationally, emotionally, magically. The shipwreck in *The Tempest*, though realistic in the first scene, is revealed by Prospero to be as contrived and as stylized a fabrication as the opening of *Lycidas* with its exordium, its questioning of the pagan deities. Each of Shakespeare's plays proceeds to raise questions of insoluble perplexity and resolves them through some final, irrational improbability, plausible only from an artful mingling of technique and imaginative reassurance which surpersedes, without even troubling to satisfy, the rational questions posed earlier. In the same way, the apotheosis of *Lycidas* forces the conclusion to affirmation where Phoebus' reply failed to satisfy the poet's complaints, and St Peter himself could only respond with an angry diatribe and a riddle. False surmise, Milton's masque-like interlude of the flowers, melts not into thin air (like Prospero's interrupted vision of the Masque of Hymen), but into the sea, the lamentation for the cruel wash of the waves over the dead man's bones. Yet it is this purely human lamentation that brings relief, like Leontes' grief of which Paulina says he cannot pay enough. 'It is required/ You do awake your faith' at the end of *Lycidas* as in Act v of *The Winter's Tale*.

Both Milton's pastoral elegy and Shakespeare's pastoral romances show us the poetic imagination playing over the central problems of life in their most abstracted forms. Shakespeare and Milton are, after all, not poles apart, but much closer than either is to the non-poet. Shakespeare's enormous influence on English literature, perhaps because of all poets he is the least formal and prescriptive, has proved more diffuse and vital than that of the great in most other countries. In an age of neo-classicism it kept open the idea that there was 'always an appeal from the rules to nature', and it was never confined to one particular genre. That the greatest English Renaissance poet should also have been a genius in character creation was an accident of supreme importance to the future of English literature. Novelists as much as poets—and both more than dramatists—inherited and were able to use something of the quality of his vision. Milton himself, more firmly rooted in Renaissance

and classical convention than Shakespeare, learned from him
what cannot be simply illustrated by verbal echoes or even the
influence of imagery. His view of human nature was to a great
extent, I believe, affected by his reading of Shakespeare.

It is generally acknowledged that in his early poetry Milton
shows a Renaissance abundance and a subtlety of imagination
which enriched his idiosyncratic and opinionated view of human
life. But it is often maintained that this phase was soon eclipsed
in the political and religious disputes of the Civil War, and that the
impressive verbal and formal architecture of *Paradise Lost* entailed
a rejection or a sacrifice of the sources that had originally nourished
it. There are, however, Shakespearian allusions in both *Samson
Agonistes* and *Paradise Regained* whose effect might persuade us to
modify this view.

In *Samson Agonistes*, whatever date we assign to it, we have a
play that could not be further from the Elizabethan drama with
which Milton was familiar. Yet it contains two recollections of
Shakespeare which have not so far claimed any critical attention,
but which seem to me to be as illuminating as the echo in *Lycidas*.
When Manoah hears of Samson's death he falls instinctively into a
Shakespearian style of speech—a passage where the images read
like a brilliant parody:

> What windy joy this day had I conceived
> Hopeful of his delivery, which now proves
> Abortive as the first-born bloom of spring
> Nipped with the lagging rear of winter's frost . . .
> (*S.A.*, 1574-7)

The editors of the Longman edition cite *Love's Labour's Lost*, I.i.
100-1—'an envious-sneaping frost/That bites the first-born in-
fants of the spring'; but the lines also recall Capulet bemoaning
his daughter:

> Death lies on her like an untimely frost
> Upon the sweetest flower of all the field . . .
> (*Romeo and Juliet*, IV.v.28-9)

The old man grieving over his child came to Milton's imagination in a Shakespearian guise. Under this influence Manoah

appears as a figure of an unheroic, natural kind—a Capulet or
Polonius (which indeed his worldly advice to his son earlier suggests)—a busy, bewildered old man whose nature, like Capulet's
or Gloster's, worn-down but obstinate, unable to face the ex-
tremity of suffering with any ultimate sense of its significance, is
still capable of rallying at the crisis. Manoah's injunction: 'Nothing is here for tears, nothing to wail/Or knock the breast; no
weakness, no contempt,/Dispraise or blame, nothing but well and
fair', is only possible because he is already planning the obsequies,
envisaging the practical details of washing off the clotted blood
and building a monument and organizing future ceremonies. So,
too, Capulet describes the tragic reversal of what had promised so
fair in terms of ritual:

> All things that we ordained festival
> Turn from their office to black funeral:
> Our instruments to melancholy bells,
> Our wedding cheer to a sad burial feast,
> Our solemn hymns to sullen dirges change;
> Our bridal flowers serve for a buried corpse;
> And all things change them to the contrary.
> (R. and J., IV.v.84–90)

If Milton knew how ordinary men respond to tragedy he knew it
through Shakespeare. The tremendous Chorus: 'All is best,
though we oft doubt' with its supernatural assertions is in strong
contrast to this more human response. The difference is reflected
in the metre and style of verse, for what one great poet reveals of
his understanding of another is most often contained in the subtle
shifts of stress and accent which recall another art and attitude. The
Miltonisms of Manoah—'only bewailing/His lot unfortunate in
nuptial choice' have a ring of clumsy irony as if Milton recognized
—consciously or not—the inadequacy of this character to his own
vision. We may not laugh at the Chorus, but we may smile at
Manoah's version of 'the unsearchable dispose/Of highest wisdom'.

The same work also contains a more elaborate reference to
Shakespeare in yet another of Samson's would-be comforters,
Dalila. Her entrance described by the Chorus as 'like a stately
ship' is noted by commentators as a common Renaissance com-

parison. But the nearest association is more precise. 'With all her bravery on and tackle trim,/Sails filled and streamers waving', 'An amber scent of odorous perfume/Her harbinger, a damsel train behind', bring to mind Enobarbus' description of Cleopatra: 'The silken tackle/Swell with the touches of those flower-soft hands'; 'A strange invisible perfume hits the sense/Of the adjacent wharves'. We are meant, surely, to remember the destruction of another heroic soldier, and though the verbal echoes are discreet, the similarity of atmosphere is strong. 'Why is my Lord enraged against his love?' Cleopatra asks, and it is much the same question that Dalila puts to Samson. 'Let weakness then with weakness come to parle' might have been Cleopatra's excuse too, had Shakespeare possessed Milton's narrowly analytic sense of conflict. What Milton owes to Shakespeare here (as in *Paradise Lost*) is a human dialogue in the clash of personalities. It comes over strongly in this episode of *Samson Agonistes*; Shakespeare himself never wrote anything more moving than Samson's rejection of Dalila's overtures: 'No, no, of my condition take no care;/It fits not; thou and I long since are twain'. An attentive ear might catch in these lines an interruption of the normal Miltonic metre—the caesura coming after the second or third syllables, strong stresses hiving together at the beginning of the line—all rhythmic variations that suggest Shakespeare. Yet these allusions in *Samson* underline the differences between the two poets while they illustrate their interaction. Enobarbus' picture of Cleopatra—'the fancy's work outpiecing nature quite'—is more engaging to the intellect and the imagination and less immediately shocking to the senses than the Chorus's description of Dalila's final approach:

> Like a fair flower surcharged with dew, she weeps
> And words addressed seem into tears dissolved,
> Wetting the borders of her silken veil.
> (*S.A.*, 728–30)

Milton's is a more exclusively sensuous imagination than Shakespeare's.

Metrical variation as much as imagery or verbal imitation

betrays Milton's concern with Shakespeare at any particular point. If this is so in *Samson Agonistes* it is even more apparent in *Paradise Regained* where there is at least one direct reference to a favourite Shakespearian *topos* contained in lines that brilliantly mimic Shakespeare's speech. In this most austere and argumentative of Milton's poems the allusions lie open on the surface of the work and are surely intended to be recognized. This is manifestly true of the allusions to Spenser, like the description of Satan's first appearance which recalls Archimago in his disguise encountering Red Crosse in Book I of the *Faerie Queene:*

> But now an aged man in rural weeds,
> Following, as seemed, the quest of some stray ewe,
> Or withered sticks to gather; which might serve
> Against a winter's day when winds blow keen,
> To warm him wet returned from field at eve,
> He saw approach . . .
>
> (*P.R.,* 1.314–19)

The falsity of this pastoral figure—his 'gray dissimulation'—is quickly detected by Christ. Milton endows Christ throughout the poem with the art of seeing through every disguise, however delusive, and overthrowing in argument every commonplace, however persuasive. Satan's offer of riches leading to power and dominion is rejected by Christ in Book II, but not before he has brooded on the reasons for such a rejection, and dismissed the influence of one of the favourite themes of Shakespeare's histories —the burden of kingship.

> What if with like aversion I reject
> Riches and realms; yet not for that a crown,
> Golden in show, is but a wreath of thorns,
> Brings dangers, troubles, cares and sleepless nights
> To him who wears the regal diadem,
> When on his shoulders each man's burden lies;
> For therein stands the office of a king,
> His honour, virtue, merit and chief praise,
> That for the public all this weight he bears.
>
> (*P.R./* II.457–65)

These lines, read out of context, could easily be mistaken for Shakespeare's. They are, of course, a resumé of the gist of the three long speeches on this theme in the histories—Henry IV's and Hal's in *Henry IV Part II*, and Henry V's soliloquy before Agincourt. The tone of soliloquy pervades them and they powerfully suggest Christ inwardly brooding on the issue rather than Christ directly addressing Satan. The rhythms fall into that easy flexibility of Shakespeare's middle style, syncopated over the regular iambic beat, making us hear the clusters of unstressed syllables that counterpoint the underlying timing which are so common a feature of Shakespeare's blank verse. 'Yet not for that a crown,/Golden in show, is but a wreath of thorns'; 'that for the public all this weight he bears'. Henry V's soliloquy contains many of these: 'O hard condition/Twinborn with greatness'; 'Art thou ought else but place, degree and form?' 'I am a king that find thee, and I know . . .' In the same speech the iteration of lists is equally characteristic: 'Let us our lives, our souls/Our debts, our careful wives,/Our children and our sins lay on the King;' "Tis not the balm, the sceptre and the ball,/The sword, the mace, the crown imperial . . .' Milton recalls this trick briefly when Christ observes that the crown 'Brings dangers, troubles, cares and sleepless nights/To him who wears the regal diadem', words not readily expected from a supporter of regicide. He has reproduced Shakespeare's speech-patterns perfectly, and the ventriloquism is surely intentional. It is as if he were saying, 'Remember what Shakespeare has to say about kingship?' And then continues, 'But I am writing about a very different kind of sovereignty.' To prove it, the rhythms modulate immediately—in the next line—into the most emphatic and regular of Milton's own prosodic effects:

> Yet he who reigns within himself and rules
> Passions, desires, and fears, is more a King;
> Which every wise and virtuous man attains:
> And who attains not, ill aspires to rule
> Cities of men and headstrong multitudes,
> Subject himself to anarchy within,
> Or lawless passions in him which he serves.
>
> (*P.R.*/ II.466–72)

It is a remarkable instance of Milton's poetic virtuosity put to the service of his argument.

The final appearance of Satan after the storm in Book IV—a storm which itself contains echoes of early Shakespeare (Clarence's dream in *Richard III*) in the ghosts and furies who 'environ' Christ, howling and shrieking—presents him in a jaunty insolent mood, and there is a familiar ironic swagger in his tone which recalls Shakespeare's human fiends, Iago and Edmund:

> Fair morning yet betides thee Son of God,
> After a dismal night; I heard the rack
> As earth and sky would mingle; but myself
> Was distant, and these flaws, though mortals fear them
> As dangerous to the pillared frame of heaven,
> Or to the earth's dark basis underneath,
> Are to the main as inconsiderable,
> And harmless, if not wholesome, as a sneeze
> To man's less universe, and soon are gone . . .
>
> (*P.R.*, IV.451–9)

Milton echoes his early self here—the pillared frame and the earth's dark basis recall the very Shakespearian lines of the Elder Brother in *Comus*:

> . . . if this fail,
> The pillared firmament is rottenness,
> And earth's base built on stubble.
>
> (596–8)

But the jauntiness, the well-timed comic bathos of the harmless, wholesome sneeze are contemptuously dismissed. 'So talked he,' writes Milton, and Satan's Shakespearian tone elicits from Christ a grimly laconic answer, entirely typical of Milton: 'Me worse than wet thou find'st not'.

It is as if here in *Paradise Regained* Milton were using his poetic memories of Spenser and of Shakespeare as a short cut to certain effects that recall the flexibility, the complexity, the duplicity of the world Christ must reject. His rejection has troubled many readers. The ambivalence which in *Comus* could use the richest poetry to support the falsest arguments, is repeated here in the allusions to Milton's best-loved poets who adumbrate the things that Christ must relinquish. When Satan, with a similar ambiguity (unconscious on Milton's part, I suspect), claims to have hoped for Christ's mercy as

> A shelter and a kind of shading cool
> Interposition, as a summer's cloud . . .
> (*P.R.*, III.ii.221–2)

the faint but exact verbal echo brings back to us the tormented and haunted figure of Macbeth: 'Can such things be,/And overcome us like a summer's cloud/Without our special wonder?' Nevertheless, it is the comprehensiveness of the Shakespearian imagination that Milton seems to be withdrawing from in *Paradise Regained*, though he salutes it openly in parting. One would prefer to think that *Samson Agonistes* followed *Paradise Regained* (and the arguments assembled by modern editors for placing it before *Paradise Lost* are not conclusive), if only because it demonstrates so rich and creative a use of Milton's Shakespearian memory. If we take the traditional date for *Samson Agonistes*, we may believe that Shakespeare's imagination remained a vital source and stimulus for Milton to the end of his life.

There are no clear-cut critical conclusions to be drawn from such an exercise as I have followed here. The lack of them seems to me an argument for the value of tracing these intimate and gratuitous connections between two great poets. Pope's use of Milton's account of Satan's journey from hell to earth in *The Dunciad* affords a similar example of what one poetic imagination can derive from another in the most unlikely context. Wordsworth's unexpected verbal echoes of Spenser and his use of the old eclogue convention of the *Shepherd's Calendar* translated into contemporary terms in *The Idle Shepherd Boys* are another. In each case what we learn is not a new interpretation, but a greater awareness of the way in which the creative imagination operates which must provide us with glimpses at least, perhaps an insight, into the art and nature of poetic composition.

III

Leontes' Contrition and the Repair of Nature

ALASTAIR FOWLER

The Winter's Tale and *Measure for Measure* fall each into distinct sections written in different fictive modes. In *Measure for Measure*, the early, potentially tragic scenes of naturalism have been contrasted with the subsequent allegorical black comedy, which is supposed to show a 'falling off'. In *The Winter's Tale*, the contrast between the first three acts (again largely naturalistic) and the pastoral-comical continuation is too sharp, and the writing too good, to seem anything but intentional. Still, the marvels and unconvincing deaths have been regretted. And Rosalie Colie, doing what she could for a 'conspicuously ill-made' play,[1] has presented it as an extreme generic experiment: an essay in *genera mixta* that has perhaps not quite come off. Its tragic and comic portions are 'not articulated' but merely juxtaposed; so that genre is 'forced' (pp. 267-8), with contrary generic tendencies allowed to confront one another. *The Winter's Tale* becomes in fine a play about the problems of tragi-comedy. Now, Shakespeare was probably aware of these problems (as any literary man would be, at a time when they were the subject of prolonged controversy). But he did a good deal to articulate the disparate members. The genres may confront one another through the grotesque indecorum of the clown's nuntius speech; but other passages and brief touches—the name Sicilia, early allusions to shepherds, anticipations of the image of the storm—show an approach less abrupt. As Colie herself noticed, the oracle in Act III, Scene ii is a characteristic motif of pastoral romance.[2] But it is also a tragic

---

[1] Rosalie L. Colie, *Shakespeare's Living Art* (Princeton University Press, 1974), 266.

[2] *Ibid.* 270 (for documentation see J. H. P. Pafford's note in the New Arden edn (Methuen and Harvard University Press, 1963), which I have used for

motif: it serves in fact as a generically ambiguous feature, allowing a shading of tragedy into romance. Moreover, the play's
thematic continuity is also far stronger than most current criticism
supposes. Only, the continuous strands are symbolic and mythological in character. Modern audiences being less at home with the
non-naturalistic connections, they have not been much explored.
But in the Renaissance the deepest treatments of passions and of
ideas were quite likely to take a romance or symbolic form. This
is not to say that Shakespeare expresses his meaning through
personification allegory like that of *Old Fortunatus*. But the symbols of *The Winter's Tale* depend on allegorical relations and even
on scraps of narrative allegory. And we shall not understand the
play until we glimpse something of these allegorical lines. Their
continued metaphors dominate the last three acts, and have profound implications for their staging.

The Winter's Tale is about a man's jealousy and rage; his
gradual contrition; and his eventual repentance. We call the man
Leontes; although properly Leontes symbolizes only part of the
experience, as Polixenes symbolizes another. Both commit the
sins of jealousy and of self-righteousness. But they do so in complementary ways: Leontes' jealousy of a wife is expressed tyran-
nously, against the opinion of his court; Polixenes' jealousy of a
son takes a more disguised, perhaps more socially acceptable,
form. Jealousy bulks large in Shakespeare's work, as in the mind of
his time. But in this play it seems to figure mainly as a representative sin to be repented. The focus is less on the experience of
jealousy itself (although this is evoked, in the first two acts, with
the plausible verisimilitude of Shakespeare's art at its best) than
on its consequences. The difficulty of repentance, we may say, is
the play's subject.

Leontes' jealousy soon leads to estrangement from Hermione
and to her loss. As Shakespeare's choice of her name suggests,
this has a symbolic force. The name is not from *Pandosto*, or

---

Winter's Tale quotations and references). Earlier pastoral features include the
place name *Sicilia*; similes from shepherding such as I.ii.1 ff. ('the shepherd's
note') and I.ii.67 ff. ('twinned lambs'). Romance features include the bear, exposure of Perdita and the shipwreck (III.iii).

from Plutarch. Hermione was anciently the daughter of Menelaus and Helen.[1] But by one of those heuristic confusions which make Renaissance mythology subtly yet profoundly different from its pagan counterpart, she was identified by Stephanus and others with Harmonia, daughter of Jupiter and Electra (or of Mars and Venus). The two names became alternative forms; so that Milton could make Hermione, not Harmonia, the wife of Cadmus.[2] At their marriage, he tells us, 'all the choirs of heaven sang in concert'.[3] This universal celebration was appropriate because Renaissance interpreters took Hermione–Harmonia to refer to the Pythagorean harmony of the moral or cosmic order. The way in which Hermione was thought of in the early seventeenth century is probably well exemplified by George Sandys's Commentary on Ovid *Metamorphoses* IV:

> Cadmus, after so many difficulties, advanced to a flourishing kingdom (Honour is to be courted with sweat and blood, and not with perfumes and garlands) now seemeth happy in his exile: having besides Harmione to wife; whose nuptials were honoured by the presence of the Gods, and their bountiful endowments. So beloved of them is the harmony of exterior and interior beauty espoused to Virtue. She is said to be the daughter of Mars and Venus; in that music not only recreates the mind with a sweet oblivion of former misfortunes, but also inflames it with courage . . .[4]

If Hermione signifies the soul's harmony, her loss would aptly symbolize Leontes' sinful state of psychological discord. The cos-

[1] Hermione was also a town with a famous cult of Ceres and Proserpina. On the statue of special importance in Ceres' cult, see Vicenzo Cartari, *Imagini delli Dei de gl' Antichi* (Venice, 1647), 121, 125.

[2] *Paradise Lost*, IX.503–6, 'not those that in Illyria changed/Hermione and Cadmus'. On the confusion of Hermione and Harmonia, see D. T. Starnes and E. W. Talbert, *Classical Myth and Legend in Renaissance Dictionaries* (University of North Carolina, 1955), 243.

[3] *Prolusion* 2; Yale Prose Milton, I.238. See, e.g., Diodorus Siculus, V.49; Ovid *Met.*, III.132; Apollodorus, *Bibliotheca*, III.iv.2; Natale Conti, *Mythologiae*, IX.14.

[4] George Sandys, *Ovid's Metamorphosis Englished, Mythologized and Represented in Figures* (1632), 99.

mic significance, the order of nature, is implied in the original righteousness whose loss the individual sin recapitulates. To find so large a meaning in Hermione's absence seems not unreasonable, in view of the play's many universalizing speeches with religious overtones:

They looked as they had heard of a world ransomed, or one destroyed . . .   (v.ii.14–15)

if all the world could have seen 't, the woe had been universal.
                                                                    (v.ii.90–1)

To regard such speeches merely as burlesque of court hyperbole is to underestimate the closeness of construction. A series of such overtones—not all from First and Second Gentlemen—culminates with the statue's movement, when it is music that brings Hermione's recovery; 'Music awake her; strike' (v.ii.98). These words of Paulina's, which are far more than a conventional adjunct of the transformation scene, imply the operation of magical or moral music, the ordering principle that in Shakespeare regularly opposes the destructive storm.[1] Moral harmony has been recovered.

The juncture at which Leontes loses Hermione is when he first realizes something of his guilt. Previously, throughout the trial, he has been self-righteous. Only when he hears the oracle ('Hermione is chaste . . . Leontes a jealous tyrant') and having denied it finds it immediately confirmed by Mamillius' death, does he recognize his fault: 'Apollo's angry, and the heavens themselves/ Do strike at my injustice' (iii.ii.146–7). Meanwhile Hermione is 'dying', as the next speech, Paulina's, tells us: 'This news is mortal to the queen: look down/And see what death is doing'. Subsequently we learn that she fainted before hearing all of the oracle.[2] This sequence of events is intelligible enough as fable: the good news of the oracle's first words has been too much for Hermione.

[1] See Northrop Frye, 'Recognition in *The Winter's Tale*', reptd in *Fables of Identity* (New York: Harcourt, Brace & World, 1963), 117.
[2] iii.ii.148–9 (no s.d. in Folio); cf. v.iii.126–7, where Hermione explains that she only learnt the rest of the oracle from Paulina.

(So, when Bellaria hears the oracle in *Pandosto* she is 'surcharged
. . . with extreme joy'.) The sequence is also highly meaningful,
however, in allegorical terms; alluding to a Pauline doctrine that
profoundly influenced thinking about sin and repentance, and that
was reflected in other literary works of the period.[1] St Paul's
fullest statement is at Rom. 7.7–13:

I knew not what sin meant, but by the law. . . . I once lived
without law. But when the commandment came, sin revived
and I was dead. And the very same commandment which was
ordained unto life, was found to be unto me an occasion of
death.

This Pauline idea of a sinner's virtual death at the coming of the
divine commandment may well underlie Hermione's 'death' at the
report of the 'ear-deafening voice o' the oracle'.[2] It is, after all, a
divine commandment judging Leontes guilty. True, it is Hermione who 'dies' and not Leontes himself. But we should recall
how closely Shakespeare identifies Hermione with Leontes'
honour—'The sacred honour of himself, his queen's'[3]—and even
with his innocent soul. There is more than one sense in which
Leontes may say to Hermione 'Your actions are my dreams'.[4]

Before the oracle, the topic of innocence is developed both in
relation to Hermione and Leontes. In Act II, Scene i, for example,
Antigonus and others defend Hermione's spotless innocence at
some length. But innocence is also attributed to Leontes, and not
only by himself:

[1] See further my 'The Image of Mortality: *The Faerie Queene*, II.i–ii', *HLQ*
24 (1961), 91–110. S. L. Bethell, '*The Winter's Tale*': *A Study* (Staples, 1947), 74,
suggests that the Pauline doctrine of baptism may be involved, without going
into detail.

[2] III.i.9. See Bethell 83–4 on Shakespeare's amplification of the oracle's
sanctity.

[3] II.iii.84; cf. III.ii.43, 45, 51.

[4] III.ii.82; cf. 81, where Hermione says 'My life stands in the level of your
dreams', meaning 'within the range of your aggressive delusions', but perhaps
with a punning implication. See Nevill Coghill, 'Six Points of Stage-craft' in
Shakespeare 'The Winter's Tale': *A Casebook*, ed. K. Muir (Macmillan, 1968),
212.

POL. We were as twinned lambs that did frisk i' th' sun,
And bleat the one at th' other: what we changed
Was innocence for innocence: we knew not
The doctrine of ill-doing, nor dreamed
That any did. Had we pursued that life,
And our weak spirits ne'er been higher reared
With stronger blood, we should have answered heaven
Boldly 'not guilty', the imposition cleared
Hereditary ours.   (I.ii.67–75)

Polixenes playfully attributes temptation to womankind: 'Temptations have since then been born to 's: for/In those unfledged days was my wife a girl' (I.ii.77–8). And behind this amiable flirtation, we might catch a hint of nostalgia for male friendship, a dubious innocence of 'twinned lambs', a simple concord before the disturbance of heterosexuality. Moreover, it is a mistaken application of Hermione's reply ('If you first sinned with us . . . that you slipped not/With any but with us'), to Polixenes alone rather than to the generality of husbands including himself, that in all probability occasions Leontes' jealousy; so that his sinful action may begin with illusory innocence. Moreover, possessive love of his friend seems to occasion pique in Leontes when it is Hermione who persuades Polixenes to stay in Sicilia.[1] And Paulina's remark about 'Fancies too weak for boys, too green and idle/For girls of nine' (III.ii.181–2) also implies immaturity. But little can be made of such motivation, since Shakespeare focuses on consequences, not aetiology. Leontes' madness is an 'infection', like 'the imposition . . . Hereditary ours'—original sin—of which the dramatist clearly takes a more serious view than Polixenes.

Two distinct allegories about Leontes' sin might be disengaged: (1) an allegory about harmony, with Hermione representing a state of mind lost and recovered; and (2) an allegory about guilt's virtual death, with Hermione as the soul that dies. These meanings are not logically compatible. But then, The Winter's Tale is not

[1] See the balanced consideration of motives in A. D. Nuttall, Shakespeare: 'The Winter's Tale', Studies in English Literature, 26 (Arnold, 1966), 24, et pass.

simple allegory. Its symbolism can imply both aspects of sin (if no more) without contradiction.

Besides the apparent death of Hermione, Leontes' sin and judgment are accompanied by a series of unreversed mortalities: the dwindling death of Mamillius, the sudden death of Antigonus, the drowning of the mariners who carried Perdita to Bohemia. Northrop Frye treats the deaths as sacrificial.[1] But they are more intelligible if we regard them as objectifying particular aspects of sin. Thus, news of Mamillius' death marks the beginning of Leontes' remorse. Apollo's revelations seem at first to leave Leontes unaffected ('There is no truth at all i' th' Oracle'); but knowledge of Mamillius' death instantly brings guilt ('Apollo's angry'). Leontes realizes, that is to say, the loss of innocence. The circumstances of the death confirm this interpretation. Mamillius died, according to Leontes,

> Conceiving the dishonour of his mother!
> He straight declined, dropped, took it deeply,
> Fastened and fixed the shame on 't in himself,
> Threw off his spirit, his appetite, his sleep,
> And downright languished.   (II.iii.13–17)

And according to a servant Mamillius died 'with mere conceit [thought] and fear' of the verdict on Hermione (III.ii.144–5). While these explanations are not impossible, the death is more eloquent as a symbolic statement: innocence dwindles with growing consciousness of sin. Mamillius' touching innocence, particularly in his scene with the ladies (II.i), is his main trait. But he also incorporates Leontes' dynastic hopes of natural perpetuity. As his heir, an 'unspeakable comfort', he 'physics' the nation with 'the hopes of him' (I.i.34 ff.). More than once, he is called a 'hopeful' prince (III.ii.41; cf. II.iii.85). But when Leontes loses the best of his natural life (the first-born), his hope of immortality is gone. He is himself under judgment of death.

The loss of an entire ship's company in the storm of III.iii seems more cut-and-dried allegory. Yet this disaster has been called 'morally and dramatically unnecessary': unsporting, so to say, on

[1] 'Recognition in *The Winter's Tale*', 112.

Shakespeare's part.[1] We are assured that 'in performance their deaths hardly evoke pity or terror'. Certainly the clown's narration encourages neither: he cuts with breathless gusto from sea tragedy to land tragedy, making the heaped disasters tragi-comic by mere excess. But Shakespeare subsequently glosses the catastrophe at v.ii, where Third Gentleman remarks that 'all the instruments which aided to expose the child were even then lost when it was found' (v.ii.70–2). In short, the mariners are 'instruments', or instrumental causes, of Leontes' sinful rejection of grace.[2] More specifically, the finding of grace for contrition requires destruction of sin's instrumental causes; so that if Perdita has not been found the mariners need not have died. Hence Shakespeare's repeated close connection of 'things dying' with 'things new-born' (iii.iii.113): they are related aspects of repentance. And the vividly described storm that kills the mariners is allegorically identical with the 'storm perpetual' of Leontes' penance, which according to Paulina will be insufficient to move the gods. Even this episode, however, is not simply allegorical: shipwreck was too familiar an emblem of moral failure not to have something of this sense, in a scene immediately after judgment on Leontes.

Antigonus, who is simultaneously eliminated, must also be categorized as an instrumental cause, albeit reluctant, of Perdita's rejection. Indeed, his very name ('against offspring') implies a less than favourable destiny, in a play where innocence and grace are identified with the new life of Leontes' children. However, Antigonus' character is sufficiently developed, and the means of his death bizarre enough, for him to merit separate treatment. His pursuit by the bear, whose dinner he later provides, is indeed an interpretative crux. Opportunistic use of a tame bear, conveniently available at the Southwark bear-pit (Quiller-Couch); transition from tragedy to comedy through a frisson of horror succeeded by laughter at a disguised clown (Coghill); abandonment of the usual dramatic persuasion to belief, and shift to 'an

---

[1] Pafford lix, note 4.

[2] On the 'causes' of sin in seventeenth-century logic, see Leon Howard, '"The Invention" of Milton's "Great Argument": A Study of the Logic of "God's Ways to Men"', *HLQ* 9 (1945).

entirely different mode, that of romance' (Colie): prolonged
debate has not produced a solution worthy of the dramatist. An
initial frisson of horror, well achieved in the 1969 R.S.C. produc-
tion, may be the right effect for the bear. It surely draws, like the
'ever-angry bears' of *The Tempest* I.ii.289, on a common emblem
of rage.[1] As such, it is yet another 'cause' of Leontes' sin: the
formal (i.e. his sin takes the *form* of jealous rage). It too must therefore be eliminated. Thus, the bear does not merely happen by, but
is being hunted—'This is the chase' (III.iii.57). To arrange for the
bear to kill Antigonus *en passant* is economical plotting, and not at
all the unnecessary complication Quiller-Couch thought it. But
the arrangement is also ironic; since Antigonus earlier expressed a
naïve trust in nature's kindness, when he accepted Leontes'
commission:

> Some powerful spirit instruct the kites and ravens
> To be thy nurses! Wolves and bears, they say,
> Casting their savageness aside, have done
> Like offices of pity.　　　　　　　　　(II.iii.185–8)

The bear, sometimes a symbol of the dangerous aspect of *prima
materia*,[2] could figure as an emblem of nature, considered in
opposition to man's constructive efforts. It is thus related to
themes of nature and art that some have seen as the play's main
concern.

The prayer of Antigonus may be a pious allusion to the story
of Elisha and the ravens. But it is also more distinctly an allusion

[1] See Pierio Valeriano, *Hieroglyphica* (Lyons, 1595), 106. Cf. Peele *Old Wives'
Tale*, 196–202, 'he with his chanting spells/Did turn me straight unto an ugly
bear ... And all the day I sit, as now you see,/And speak in riddles, all inspired
with rage,/Seeming an old and miserable man:/And yet I am in April of my
age'; Nashe, *The Unfortunate Traveller*, in *Works*, ed. McKerrow and Wilson,
2 (Oxford: Blackwell, 1958), 240, 'a bear (which is the most cruelest of all
beasts)'. The comedy of the scene is no argument (*pace* Pafford 72 note) against
its having allegorical contents; particularly in view of the didactic theory that
favoured incongruous fables. On the use of bizarre images, see E. H. Gombrich,
Symbolic Images (Phaidon, 1972), 123–95: 'Icones symbolicae'. R. G. Hunter,
Shakespeare and the Comedy of Forgiveness (New York and London: Columbia,
1965), 192, 196 notices the iconographical appropriateness of the bear, but sees
no allegory.

[2] C. G. Jung, *Psychology and Alchemy* (Routledge, 1953), 179.

by Shakespeare himself, with a very different implication, to a later verse in 2 Kgs.2. Verse 24 relates how at Elisha's curse 'there came forth two she bears out of the wood, and tare forty and two children of them'. Following St Jerome (in Ps. 108) and St Isidore (*Glossa ordinaria*), commentators interpreted this passage as referring to God's expectation of repentance by the Jews, after the death of Christ, for 42 years. Only then, when conversion was not forthcoming, did he send the Roman Vespasian and Titus to destroy Jerusalem. The bear, then, specifically symbolizes God's judgment on reluctance to repent.

Antigonus' pietism and his (rather *ex parte*) application of the Bible should not mislead us into thinking him a martyr, or an example of true faith. On the contrary, Shakespeare repeatedly contrasts him with Paulina and Camillo in this regard. Kindly but ineffectual, Antigonus has a conventional inclination to obey his sovereign right or wrong. Of course Shakespeare exploits the comic possibilities of a weak husband impotent to silence his wife, and involves the audience on Antigonus' side ('Hang all the husbands/That cannot . . .'). But this should not conceal Antigonus' fault in *trying* to silence Paulina. Moreover, he is prepared to buy the tyrant off with promises. In a sense he is even accessory to Leontes' crimes. The way in which he echoes Leontes' errors (though in a harmless form) comes out in his ludicrous but revealing response to the idea of Hermione's guilt. If she is 'honour-flawed', his own daughters will suffer for it, he promises, in lines that substantiate his sinister name:

> By mine honour
> I'll geld 'em all; fourteen they shall not see
> To bring false generations: they are co-heirs,
> And I had rather glib myself, than they
> Should not produce fair issue.   (II.i.146–50)

It is a coarse, comic horsey transposition of the same obsession with honour and 'fair issue' that Leontes—and Polixenes—display. Later, Antigonus acts 'against generation'—and against faith in Hermione's innocence—when a vision convinces him of her guilt, and he accepts its directive to expose the baby 'upon the earth/ Of its right father' Polixenes (III.iii.45–6). This scene sifts the quality of the audience's faith too: they have every reason, almost, for saying with Antigonus 'I do believe/Hermione hath suffered death', and to that extent interpreting the vision similarly. Only the simply devout, perhaps, are untroubled, content to have seen providence in the dream's selection of Bohemia.

Eventually Antigonus is succeeded as Paulina's spouse by a very different 'honourable husband'. Camillo resembles Antigonus in being kind. And he is repeatedly connected with the idea of honour.[1] But his honesty strikes us as altogether deeper and more severe. It is also more uncompromising. Camillo's 'policy' contrasts sharply with Antigonus' compliant propitiation of Leontes. *He* would have known how to break a promise to do evil.[2]

Just as the play's deaths adumbrate allegorical suggestions, so does the intrigue—for that is what it amounts to—of Paulina. As in *Measure for Measure*, the final reconciliation is elaborately stage-managed so as to bring the characters who are in the dark to a very particular spiritual state. Paulina conceals Hermione for sixteen years, and then reveals her in the form of a statue whose coming to life precipitates the *denouement*, in the play's climactic, and arguably its strongest, scene.

Hermione's concealment and vivification make a strikingly discontinuous fable. The audience is never precisely told why Hermione should allow Leontes to mourn her death, year after year, for sixteen years. Of course any rapid switch to easy reconciliation would have been unthinkable—

> When you shall come to clearer knowledge . . .
> You scarce can right me throughly, then, to say
> You did mistake.   (II.i.97–100)

But to make this a motive for sentencing Leontes to sixteen years' grief and penance would be to make Hermione a monster. And to say that

---

[1] III.ii.165–70 'He (most humane/And filled with honour) . . . himself commended,/No richer than his honour'; cf. I.ii.310, 407, 410, 442; II.ii.188; IV.iv.511; V.i.193.

[2] Hunter 195 shows that according to the moral theology of Shakespeare's time Antigonus would not be thought bound by an evil oath.

a major part of any cure for her must consist of the knowledge
that Leontes had been purified. . . . Forgiveness must be won:
it cannot be given where there is any suspicion of unworthi-
ness[1]

is theologically unsound (no man is worthy) and in any case inconsistent with Hermione's character. Such a grudging censorious
calculation of worthiness is not in her free nature. (Leontes speaks
of her at I.ii.102–5 as having been stiff in courtship; but that is
probably only Shakespeare's conventional sign of her virtue.)
Nor does it seem like Hermione to stand as a statue withholding
every sign of emotion, during Leontes' exclamations. The en-
livening of the statue is presented as a miracle requiring faith
(v.iii.95); so that we should perhaps not expect a full explanation.
There may even be a sense in which Hermione has been dead and
brought to life again. After all, for many of the audience the
evidence that she died has been firm and uncontroverted. Indeed,
Paulina almost affirms it on oath at III.ii.203: 'I say she's dead: I'll
swear 't. If word nor oath/Prevail not, go and see'.[2] Few notice
that she does not actually swear. And it is hard to think of anything in the subtext that can have emptied such speeches of their
weight. Hermione never appears during the interval between her
faint and the transformation—after which Leontes remains
baffled: 'I saw her,/As I thought, dead'. In fact, the discontinuity
is so marked, the undramatic irony so extreme, that the audience
are 'as . . . mocked with art'.

The possibility that Shakespeare was indifferent to continuity
has not deterred those bent on finding psychological causes.
Coleridge remarked that

it seems a mere indolence of the great bard not to have provided
in the oracular response . . . some ground for Hermione's

---

[1] Pafford lxix.
[2] Many passages confirm the impression: e.g. III.iii.16–46 (Antigonus' vision
of Hermione's ghost, which leads him to say 'I do believe/Hermione hath
suffered death') and v.iii.115–17: 'That she is living,/Were it but told
you, should be hooted at/Like an old tale'; III.ii.201; III.iii.42; v.i.80; v.iii.
140.

seeming death and fifteen [*sic*] years' voluntary concealment. This might have been easily effected by some obscure sentence of the oracle, as for example:—'Nor shall he ever recover an heir, if he have a wife before that recovery.'[1]

Quiller-Couch followed Coleridge, and others such as Gervinus, over-ingenious in their naturalism, went a step further and imagined the change in the oracle actually effected. So now it is often supposed that Hermione's motive really is a wish not to offend Apollo, or not to spoil Leontes' chance of an heir.[2] We need to remind ourselves of the oracle as Shakespeare gives it: merely that 'the king shall live without an heir, if that which is lost be not found' (III.ii.134–6). Nothing about Leontes and Hermione cohabiting. As for Hermione's 'explanation', all that she says is:

> thou shalt hear that I,
> Knowing by Paulina that the Oracle
> Gave hope thou wast in being, have preserved
> Myself to see the issue.[3]

This by no means explains why she did not reveal herself earlier (even if Leontes and she had to avoid conceiving an heir).

The apparently cruel intrigue might be more amenable to explanation in generic terms. *The Winter's Tale* has many romance features (as its name leads us to expect);[4] and romances after

---

[1] *Shakespearean Criticism*, ed. T. M. Raysor, 2 vols. (Dent, 1960), I.119.

[2] G. G. Gervinus, *Shakespeare Commentaries*, tr. F. E. Bunnett (1883), 811; Bethell 87, 102.

[3] v.iii.125–8; This is treated by Pafford as a loose end, since Hermione was present herself to hear the oracle; but see n. 8 above on the timing of Hermione's faint. The speech is probably allegorical: Hermione knew by Paulina's theological instruction that there was hope of grace (i.e., of Perdita's recovery).

[4] Frye 107 takes 'winter's tale' to refer to the dark first part of the play. But *winter's tale* seems to have been used either as a generic term for a fairy-tale or romance; or else in the sense 'fantastic, idle tale'. So examples in *OED* s.v. *Winter* 5: 'A mere winter-story without any ground or reason'; 'Old wives' fables and winter tales'; 'Such winter tales as it were too great a mispence of time and words to refute them'.

all are full of extreme, irrational actions, unmotivated or inade-
quately motivated. Behaviour in them may seem to us almost
psychopathological; as when, to cite a familiar instance, the
Count of Ponthieu's daughter, having been raped, tries to murder
her quite innocent husband, who has been defending her. Such
actions were beyond the reach of rational understanding, but not
necessarily of fiction and of wisdom. From this point of view
Hermione's long seclusion might indicate the depth of her
humiliation and the strength of her hatred of Leontes for 'publish-
ing' her dishonour. But even in Elizabethan romance people
should be in character, unless some powerful reason overrides the
fable.

However, the last three acts of *The Winter's Tale* are allegorical
romance, or a blend of pastoral romance and morality. In such a
form, continuity sometimes depends entirely on the *significatio* or
allegory. And in morality terms, the story is exclusively one of
Leontes' repentance. There can be no question of Paulina's and
Hermione's waiting for him to seem worthy—'There is none
worthy,/Respecting her that's gone' (v.i.34)—for the delay is not
theirs but Leontes'. It is he who cannot recover his inner harmony
until he has repented fully. It is he who is spiritually 'dead'. Thus
Hermione withdraws without any motive, involuntarily. Indeed,
as Leontes' internal harmony, she simply does not exist, until the
final scene. Her non-existence or virtual death, during the 'wide
gap' of time (iv.i.7), obviates motive. The duration of the gap
says nothing about Hermione: it has the effect, rather, of amplify-
ing the difficulty of repentance.

Shakespeare treats Leontes' repentance with unusual fulness;
unfolding it by slow stages of attrition, contrition and repentance.[1] Throughout, the sinner is directed by Paulina, who oper-

---

[1] *OED* s.v. *Attrition* cites Tucker: 'Three stages in the passage from vice to
virtue: attrition, contrition, and repentance'. Hooker defines attrition as
'horror of sin through fear of punishment, without any loving sense, or taste of
God's mercy'. Its sorrow for sin was incomplete; so that Bradford (1555) made
it 'one of the differences between contrition and attrition', that in the former
there was 'just and full' sorrow (*Works*, Parker Soc., p. 46). Shakespeare's use
of semi-technical theological terms is noticeable: see e.g. iii.ii.223 'affliction';
iii.ii.240–1 'recreation', 'exercise'; v.iii.145 'justified'.

ates as a presiding genius of justification by faith. Her ascendancy
—at first violent, but soon repentantly softened—begins with
Leontes' first admission of guilt, at the news of Mamillius' death.
Leontes' response might be thought repentant: so Pafford says
'he immediately repents' (p.lxviii); while Hunter has it that
Leontes 'immediately experiences contrition'. If his first response
is mere 'attrition', or horror of judgment ('the heavens . . . Do
strike'), surely his later public confession and promise to make
amends (III.ii.153–72: 'I'll reconcile me to Polixenes,/New woo
my queen . . .') amount to 'contrition', or full sorrow? Yet when
Paulina returns from sequestering the queen, she continues the
stage of attrition; wearing Leontes down with reminders of
judgment and counsels of despair:

> Do not repent these things, for they are heavier
> Than all thy woes can stir: therefore betake thee
> To nothing but despair.   (III.ii.208–10)

Has Leontes been too glib in his remorse? Certainly Shakespeare
makes much of Paulina's memorial function; giving it comic
development when she repeatedly breaks her promise not to
remind Leontes of his losses: 'I'll not remember you of my own
lord/(Who is lost too)' (III.ii.230–1). After sixteen years she is
still tactlessly reminding him—as at v.i.15 ('she you killed')—
when events trap her in having to steer him away from a second
marriage. But then, after sixteen years his reconciliation with
Polixenes remains theoretical: the visit that he 'justly owes' (I.i.6–
7) has never been made. Besides, it may be wrong to think of
Paulina as keeping Hermione from Leontes. She encouraged him
from the beginning to visit, even to kiss, the 'dead' Hermione: 'go
and see: if you can bring/Tincture, or lustre in her lip, her eye'
(III.ii.204–5). Perhaps it is precisely Leontes' slowness to accept the
invitation, and to rouse his soul, that delays reunion. Even in the
transformation scene, he shows such hesitancy that Paulina must
chide him (v.iii.107). It is as if he repented only intellectually or
formally in Act III. The ordering and moving of the emotions,
however, require repeated symbolic statements and enactments

that progressively involve Leontes and the audience more and
more, until the strange ritual of the transformation brings release.
This long and painful process accords with the gravity of Shakespeare's treatment of repentance in other late plays, and contrasts
with the instant conversions in such contemporary tragi-comedies
as *Philaster*.

The final stage of Leontes' repentance coincides with the animation of Hermione: an episode in the tradition of epiphanic un-
veiling of statues in sixteenth-century *tableaux vivants* (itself related to the religious veneration of statues). An old form for an
old tale; although it would scarcely be possible to find an earlier
statue that *moved*.[1] The preceding comment scene, rightly prized
by Coghill, gives a lead in to the symbolism of the transformation
scene itself. Third Gentleman says that when Perdita heard
Hermione's death

> bravely confessed and lamented by the king . . . she did . . . I
> would fain say, bleed tears, for I am sure my heart wept blood.
> Who was most marble, there changed colour; some swooned,
> all sorrowed: if all the world could have seen 't, the woe had
> been universal. (v.ii.87–91)

In this shared movement of feeling, even in those 'most marble',
the softening of stone is the softening of hard stony hearts. We
are led to expect similar emotion in connection with the statue.
When he sees it, Leontes applies Third Gentleman's metaphor to
his own stoniness: 'I am ashamed: does not the stone rebuke me/
For being more stone than it?' (v.iii.37–8). The Biblical allusion[2]
is to the same text that underlies *Paradise Lost* XI.3–5:

---

[1] George R. Kernodle, *From Art to Theatre* (Univ. of Chicago, 1944), 62;
Inga-Stina Ewbank, 'The Triumph of Time', in Muir, 115, n. 15 (suggesting
that Shakespeare may have started a fashion for moving statues in masques).
There is a *speaking* statue in Peele's *Old Wives' Tale*.

[2] Ezek.11.19: 'And I will give them one heart, and I will put a new spirit
within you; and I will take the stony heart out of their flesh, and will give them
an heart of flesh'. Hab. 2.10–11, the text usually cited, is also apt: 'Thou hast . . .
sinned against thy soul. For the stone shall cry out of the wall, and the beam out
of the timber shall answer it.'

Prevenient grace descending had removed
The stony from their hearts, and made new flesh
Regenerate grow instead, that sighs now breathed . . .

For Leontes, then, the movable statue signifies a potentiality of
repentant emotion (*movere*). Since the death of Antigonus—who
could not weep, in spite of Hermione's injunction, in his vision,
that he should do so (III.iii.32 and 51)—the heart has been ready to
soften. But it never does, until Leontes visits Paulina's house. The
significance of the occasion is emphasized by the use of religious
words, which only have to be taken literally to disclose the allegorical meaning. Paulina describes the visit, in the language of the
court, as 'a surplus of grace' (v.iii.7). Later, when the animation is
to be attempted, she calls for spiritual response from Leontes: 'It
is required/You do awake your faith' (v.iii.94–5). By now the
softened Hermione is weeping, as her first speech shows:

> You gods, look down,
> And from your sacred vials pour your graces
> Upon my daughter's head!

—and the audience should know, by the movement of their own
feelings, that Leontes' contrition is complete. He has at last responded to the grace of repentence, and is reconciled.

Leontes' all-important condescending visit to Paulina's house,
we should notice, has little to do with his volition. Its occasion is
Perdita's wish to learn through Giulio Romano's art what her
mother was like.[1] It depends, therefore, on her return. Leontes'
recovery of Perdita precedes the softening of his heart and the
animation of Hermione, just as the rejection of Perdita preceded
the hardening of his heart and Hermione's death. The oracle is
explained: what Leontes has found is grace, prevenient grace,
grace to repent. Both Perdita and Hermione are repeatedly associated with grace. But their allegorical aspects are distinct. Perdita
is Hermione's daughter, as the descendant or successor of original
righteousness is grace to repent—'Dear queen', says Perdita, 'that

[1] v.ii.93–103; v.iii.13–14.

ended when I but began' (v.iii.45). However, the soul reanimated by repentance cannot recover its original innocence—'You scarce can right me throughly'. The twice-born Hermione is not 'tender/ As infancy and grace' (v.iii.27) but an experienced, wrinkled form.

The transformation scene has been faulted for its contrivance, staginess and inadequacy of dramatic means. But Coghill has rightly defended its fine stagecraft; especially the exquisite delay in discovering the statue's nature—which continues in a hesitation just before her first movement.[1] For Coghill, the naming of Giulio Romano as the sculptor is to borrow authenticity from the 'real' cultural world: to 'confer a special statueishness'. And Rosalie Colie reminds us of Giulio's contemporary reputation for 'miraculous illusionism'.[2] Shakespeare's own art shows its capacity for illusionism in Paulina's references to the fresh paint of the statue. This wet paint is cosmetic art in the actor's real world, Giulio's art in the second-order fictive world of Hermione's charade, but real tears in her own. (It is characteristic of Shakespeare to turn possible shortcomings of an actor to good account— imperfect stillness of the statue passes as a *vraisemblable* sign of Hermione's emotion.) But the *paragone* of arts, or of nature and art, is abandoned at a crucial point. Hermione's wrinkles are less a *tour de force* of realism (Giulio's and Shakespeare's own) than an acknowledgment of the limits of art, the claims of reality. As Rosale Colie finely puts it, the pathos of the wrinkles makes all questions about mimesis seem trivial; and 'by calling attention to the *vraisemblable* wrinkles, the playwright underscores his *invraisemblable*, and turns us back to rethink the convention of the "marvelous" in pastoral drama, the taming of a miracle to literary device' (p. 281). At the same time, the wrinkles are also an occasion of comedy: Leontes' noticing them obliges Paulina to think on her feet:

> So much the more our carver's excellence,
> Which lets go by some sixteen years and makes her
> As she lived now.   (v.iii.30–2)

[1] Coghill 212.   [2] *Shakespeare's Living Art* 280.

We are not to dwell too lugubriously on the reflection that the most excellent art shows most of nature's faults.

Shakespeare has already taken us beyond the *paragone* of nature and art to the idea of 'art/That nature makes' (IV.iv.91–2). But to understand the function of art in the transformation, we must go beyond even Polixenes' sophisticated naturalism, to a deeper view of art's place in a fallen world. This view was quite orthodox in Shakespeare's time. And it can be illustrated from a work he certainly knew, Thomas Wilson's *Art of Rhetoric*. After the Fall, writes Wilson,

> whereas man through reason might have used order: man through folly fell into error. And thus for lack of skill, and for want of grace evil so prevailed, that the devil was most esteemed. . . . Even now when man was thus past all hope of amendment, God still tendering his own workmanship, stirring up his faithful and elect, to persuade with reason all men to society . . . being somewhat drawn, and delighted with the pleasantness of reason, and the sweetness of utterance.[1]

Wilson represents 'art and eloquence' as drawing men back to the original order of human nature. Since the dramatist's art similarly worked to repair nature, the artificial character of the transformation scene is perhaps thematic in an unsuspected way. Hermione turned statue may be soul restored by art. To move, after all, is the perfection of the sculptor's Pygmalion art. The transformation would in that case be no 'outrageous device' (Colie) but moving drama—a scene meant to move the audience themselves. A common Elizabethan defence of the stage was to instance criminals and tyrants (such as Alexander of Pherae) brought to sudden repentance by a tragedy. From Leontes' point of view, moreover, the dramatist's art symbolizes that of repentance, whose *paragone* is with wrinkles—sufferings never to be made up for without grace beyond the natural. The shortcomings of art, even the possibility of excessive artificiality, are not forgotten. Too much art could be seen as impeding Hermione's movement; just as

[1] Ed. G. H. Mair (Oxford: Clarendon, 1909), 'The Preface'; cf. Frye 117.

Leontes, encouraged by Paulina, takes his penitence to what Cleomenes considers are excessive lengths.[1]

Leontes' sixteen-year repentance takes place off stage; being narrated in Time's prologue speech, Act IV, Scene i. This used also to be regarded as a clumsy 'device' (Quiller-Couch), a mere programme note, 'not central at all' (Bethell). But as *Pericles* shows, Shakespeare could leap over wide gaps of time without apology, when he wished. And Inga-Stina Ewbank has argued that Time presents himself more significantly, as a 'principle and power'.[2] This power goes beyond the revealing of truth—the aspect of time treated, nominally, in Shakespeare's main source *Pandosto* (subtitled *The Triumph of Time*. . . . Temporis filia veritas).[3] From Leontes' point of view, Time's revealing movement has so far been destructive, though just. But, as William Blisset has taught us to see, *The Winter's Tale* has the structure of a diptych, with the devouring Time of the first panel exactly matched by the redeeming Time of the second; with the turning point at the centre, Act III, Scene iii, where the devouring beast and storm symbolize 'a time of tyranny and the tyranny of time'.[4] And now, beyond the worst, beyond tragedy, Time says:

> Your patience this allowing,
> I turn my glass, and give my scene such growing
> As you had slept between: (IV.i.15–17)

We have to learn patience as well as Leontes.[5] As we do, we begin

---

[1] v.i.1–23. Cf. F. D. Hoeniger 'The Meaning of *The Winter's Tale*', *UTQ* 20 (1950), 25 on the ambivalence of art, as a source both of decadence and of creation.

[2] 'The Triumph of Time', esp. 104 ff.

[3] *Pandosto. The Triumph of Time. Wherein is discovered by a pleasant History, / that although by the means of sinister fortune, Truth may be concealed yet by Time in spite of fortune it is most manifestly revealed. Pleasant for age to avoid drowsy thoughts, profitable for youth to eschew other wanton pastimes, and bringing to both a desired content.* Temporis filia veritas. . . . On Time as a revealer, see Erwin Panofsky, *Studies in Iconology* (New York: Harper, 1962), 82–3; Fritz Saxl, '*Veritas Filia Temporis*' in *Philosophy and History: Essays Presented to Ernst Cassirer*, ed. R. Klibansky and H. J. Paton (1936), 197–222.

[4] W. Blisset, 'This Wide Gap of Time: *The Winter's Tale*', *ELR* 1 (1971), 52–69, esp. 56–9, 63.

[5] See John Taylor, 'The Patience of *The Winter's Tale*', *EC* 23 (1973), 333–56.

to see a different movement: construction and growth and change:
'things new born' replacing 'things dying' (iii.iii.112–13). Time
prepares us to understand this by his presenter's speech. For example, he three times mentions 'growth' as modified by art. It is
as if the natural course of events, 'growth untried', could be
replaced by, or grafted in with, a new order. Indeed, Time (and
not only the dramatist) claims just such a power 'To o'erthrow
law, and in one self-born hour/To plant and o'erwhelm custom'
(iv.i.8–9). It would be paltry to take these lines merely as Shakespeare's defiance of the unities. They refer to Time as a means of
change: change that can replace the order of law—the customary,
the habitual, the rigid, the hereditary world of the reprobate
Old Man—with a new order of grace. Time's 'tale' might seem
old-fashioned, or 'stale', to the taste of Shakespeare's contemporaries ('the glistering of this present') in that the device of a presenter was becoming obsolete. But in the course of the play 'the old
tale' comes to represent an object of belief, not unlike the 'old old
story' of revivalists.[1] Thus the truth that Time eventually fathers
is a vindication of faith. Indeed, in a sense Time brings forth the
faithful soul itself by a process of *conversio*: 'truth' often meant
'troth' or faithfulness.

The subtle *simplesse* of Time's presenter's speech finds matching
form in sixteen couplets corresponding to the sixteen years of
'swift passage'. We can choose to patronize this as another clumsy
device, an outmoded manner of decorum. But if we can be
patient with number symbolism, it has much to tell about the
play's structure. Of course probability dictates that Time's gap
should be more or less sixteen years: Perdita must grow to
marriageable age. But the specific choice is particularly apt for
several reasons. Precisely sixteen was given by Plato as the optimal
lower marriage age. Moreover, in certain schemes of the Ages
of Man it would bring Perdita to a stage of transition between
pueritia and *adolescentia*.[2] (In the same Varronian tradition, Leontes

---

[1] v.ii.28; v.ii.62; v.iii.115–17. Cf. Pafford liii.

[2] *De legibus* 6; see Pietro Bongo, *Numerorum mysteria* (Bergamo, 1591), 412.
Valeriano (358), partly following Varro and Censorinus, gives the five ages as:
I *infantia* (0 to 5), II *pueritia* (to 15 or 16), III *adolescentes* (to 30), IV *iuniores* (to
45), V *seniores* (from 46). Samuel C. Chew, *The Pilgrimage of Life* (Port Washing-

would also reach a transition. After the 'wide gap' he is 44 or 45, and changing from *junior* to *senior*.)[1] These references to the Ages of Man do more than glance at one of Time's measures. Transition between Ages, or phases of life, is a way of changing nature— 'growth'. The Ages were a subject of profound meditations, such as that of Plutarch on the Varronian scheme: 'dead is the man of yesterday, for he is passed into the man of today'.[2]

But the number sixteen had also a more abstract fitness to the wide gap. As a square number, and especially as the square on the tetrad, it symbolized virtue and justice. Particularly, it meant the ordering of the psyche ('Proportioned equally by seven and nine')[3] through composition of its mortal feminine part (seven) and its immortal masculine part (nine), to produce the harmony of the double octave.[4] Thus the measure of Leontes' sixteen-year repentance represents the moral *Harmonia* that he recovers. Leontes himself speaks of his repentance in a similar mathematical metaphor when he says to Paulina 'O, that ever I/Had squared me to thy counsel!'[5]

[1] For the calculation of Leontes' age, see F. W. Bateson, below, p. 70. The repeated appearance of the number 23, to which Mr Bateson draws attention, may be an intentional number symbolism. Bongo (442) comments that 'by this number can be signified the completing and perfecting of human salvation, which is brought about especially by true faith and good works. Perfect faith is denoted by the triad, which mystically implies faith in the Holy Trinity; while the perfection of works consists in observation of God's commandments, which is expressed through the number 20, in accordance with the double dyad, in that the decalogue is handed down through the Old Testament, and declared more fully in the New.'

[2] *De E apud Delph.* 292 D–E. On the general significance of the Ages of Man schemes, see Raymond Klibansky *et al.*, *Saturn and Melancholy* (Nelson, 1964), a study of the Four Ages, and the only adequate treatment of any of the schemes.

[3] Spenser, *F. Q.* II.ix.22.

[4] See my *Spenser and the Numbers of Time* (Routledge, 1964), App., esp 284 n.; also (with Douglas Brooks) 'The Structure of Dryden's *A Song for St Cecilia's Day, 1687*' in *Silent Poetry*, ed. Alastair Fowler (Routledge, 1970), 195–6, citing Macrobius, Pico and Athanasius Kircher.

[5] v.i.51–2; see *Spenser and the Numbers of Time*, 280, 287 n. Antigonus too intends to 'be squared' (regulated) by his vision's instructions (III.iii.41). But in the case of the Old Man, allegorically Leontes' sinful part, this will mean elimination.

ton, N.Y.: Kennikat, 1973), discusses the five age scheme at 160–2, 218–19, giving examples from Palingenius, Raleigh and John Davies of Hereford.

Other measures of Time are represented by more developed forms, in both the imagery and the action of the pastoral scenes; suggesting many intermingled processes of nature and art, or nature and grace.[1] Thus Perdita makes 'four-and-twenty nosegays for the shearers' (IV.iii.41). And the herdsmen's dance at the sheep-shearing feast is a dance of months or signs, almost in the symbolic manner of *ballets de cour* or masque dances. Indeed, it probably borrows the antimasque of satyrs from Jonson's *Masque of Oberon*.[2] Its mixture of nature and art could hardly therefore be more thorough: rustics disguised by art as natural satyrs perform an art-dance far from 'country art'. Shakespeare makes his added meaning obvious enough for the popular stage by repeating the numbers, under the excuse of a servant's comic prolixity: 'three carters, three shepherds, three neat-herds, three swine-herds' (IV.iv.325–6). Polixenes' amused recapitulation, 'four threes of herdsmen' makes sure that we catch the reference to months dis-posed in their seasons or signs in their humour-governing triplici-ties. Time is now ordered in its parts and ceremonially composed, where earlier it was torn apart, as between the ship's destruction and the *sparagmos* of Antigonus.

If some of the pastoral measures represent natural change, others associated with Perdita express the action of grace. Perdita des-cribes herself here as like a player in a 'Whitsun pastoral' (IV.iv.133) —the feast of Pentecost, the descent of the Holy Spirit. And most critics, including those least sympathetic to allegory,[3] agree that she embodies 'grace'; even if they take the latter as a secular analogy of grace in the Christian sense, or merely as 'graceful-ness'. Florizel's praise marvellously evokes her gracefulness, 'so singular in each particular' (IV.iv.144). But this seems to me the outward form of a distinct spiritual role that she consistently enacts throughout the overall allegory. So when Time tells us that Perdita has 'grown in grace' (IV.i.24) he implies that grace

[1] Number symbolism was a conventional feature of pastoral: see Helen Cooper, 'The Goat and the Eclogue', *PQ* 53 (1974), 372 and cf. my *Triumphal Forms* (Cambridge Univ., 1970), 139.

[2] Enid Welsford, *The Court Masque* (reissued New York: Russell & Russell, 1962), 283–4.

[3] Such as Pafford (lxxviii).

comes through a process of natural change. From this point of view Perdita's moral and spiritual value finds a highly significant reflection in her presentation of flowers at the sheepshearing feast. This ceremony too has its measures: Perdita names just sixteen species.[1]

Shakespeare further develops Perdita's meaning in terms of poetic theology. As several mythologizing critics have shown, he connects her with Proserpina, particularly in the imagery of the flower presentation.[2] Indeed, he makes Perdita apostrophize the goddess: 'O Proserpina,/For the flowers now that, frighted, thou let'st fall/From Dis's waggon!' (IV.iv.116–18). The loss and qualified return of Proserpina was a seasonal myth; but also (because of the identity of Demeter and Proserpina as different phases of growth) a theological one—a myth of death and resurrection.[3] However, another mythological *persona* of Perdita's, that seems not to have been previously discussed, is in some ways a more developed role.

Just as Hermione plays a stony-hearted statue of herself, so Perdita plays a definite part at the sheep-shearing feast: 'Flora/Peering in April's front' (IV.iv.1–2). In the Ovidian myth, which received Neoplatonic interpretations, Flora was a metamorphosis of the nymph Chloris ('Green') after her rape by Zephyrus, the quickening spirit of spring.[4] After her subsequent marriage, flowers from her garden dower, gifts of the queen of flowers, are culled by the three Horae, associated with the Graces. Perdita enacts part of this myth of the natural cycle when she presents flowers of the three ancient seasons (Horae) to her guests. From a naturalistic

---

[1] IV.iv.74–127: rosemary, rue, carnation, gillyflower, lavender, mint, savory, marjoram, marigold, daffodil, violet, primrose, oxlip, crown imperial, lily, iris.

[2] E.g. Hoeniger 22; E. A. J. Honigmann 'Secondary Sources of *The Winter's Tale*', PQ 34 (1955), 34–5.

[3] Conti v.14; x; Sandys 193. Cf. Hunter 198.

[4] *Fasti* v.195 ff. See Edgar Wind, *Pagan Mysteries in the Renaissance* (Faber, 1968), 115–17 esp. 117: 'the progression Zephyr–Chloris–Flora spells out the familiar dialectic of love. . . .' Flora's desire to count the flower colours in her garden ('saepe ego digestos volui numerare colores/nec potui') was a constant challenge to numerological imitation. On the connection of the primroses at IV.iv.122–5 with chlorosis, see Pafford 172.

standpoint, this many-seasoned passage has been baffling.[1] But in its own terms there is no uncertainty of season. The whole year is in effect covered by three groups of flowers: the 'flowers of winter' (IV.iv.79) given to Polixenes and Camillo; the 'flowers of middle summer' (IV.iv.108) given to men of middle age; and the 'flowers o' th' spring' (IV.iv.113) desiderated for Florizel, Mopsa, and the girls, who still wear upon their 'virgin branches'— branches of honour, as it were—their 'maidenheads growing'. Schemes of the Four Ages of Man related each age to a season, in just this way.[2] Shakespeare alludes to the idea unambiguously in his identification of spring with Florizel's youth (*pueritia* or *adolescentia*), summer with *virilitas* and winter with *senecta*; although he leaves the sequence incomplete, so that it could refer to three- or five-age schemes also. Spring flowers are inaccessible (IV.iv.113: 'I would I had some flowers o' th' spring, that might/ Become your time of day') for the practical reason that spring is past at sheepshearing time. But there is a more touching reason, which explains some of Perdita's melancholy at the feast. She associates flowers with girls throughout—

> primroses,
> That die unmarried, ere they can behold
> Bright Phoebus in his strength (a malady
> Most incident to maids);

—just as she herself is referred to as 'blossom' (III.iii.46). And at sixteen, Perdita is growing away from girlhood to *adolescentia* (16–30): her girlish time of day is past, and her state must change. Of course, co-presence of all the seasons would not be impossible in some earthly paradises. But in *The Winter's Tale* (unlike many pastorals) Flora's spring is conspicuously missed, and spring flowers regretted. The sense is not merely that of a vegetation myth of cyclic repair. Perdita's ritual of presentations symbolizes not only the process of natural growth, but growth associated

---

[1] As it is to Pafford (lxix, note). But he rightly rejects the popular error that the pastoral scenes take place in spring. On this point IV.iv.79, 107 and 113 are decisive. See Ewbank 108.

[2] Klibansky 293–4.

with the *Gratiae*, with grace: 'Grace and remembrance be to you both'.[1] And it is no accident that the gracious Perdita should be assisted by a shepherdess called Dorcas, after the woman 'full of good works' in Acts 9.36–9.

The other components of the pastoral scenes similarly develop themes of repair and change in the natural order and beyond it. This is obviously true of Perdita's and Polixenes' debate (IV.iv. 85–103) about the gillyflower, Puttenham's example of the power of art to 'mend nature—change it rather'.[2] Perdita's phrase 'nature's bastards' has rightly been referred to Wisd. 4.3–6, 'the multiplying brood of the ungodly shall not thrive, nor take deep rooting from bastard slips'. But the whole debate must also be seen in the context of St Paul's far more familiar development of this passage, in Rom. 11, as an allegory of election by grace and incorporation in Christ through repentance—'God is able to graff them in again'.[3] An abstract debate for country chat, it inextricably mingles art with nature, and nature with grace, in its paradoxes and nuances.

Contrary to the professed sides, as has often been pointed out, Polixenes is emotionally opposed to mixture of court and country, the grafted Perdita inclined to practise it. What matters in such things is not the side we profess. In any case, Polixenes' supposed profundity, in perceiving that horticultural art is a natural

---

[1] 'Remembrance' perhaps in a specific sense: 'Rosemary and rue signified respectively remembrance (friendship) and grace (repentance). Rue is known as 'herb grace' (Pafford). Cf. Robert Greene *Upstart Courtier* (1871), 4: 'some of them smiled and said "rue was called herb *grace*" which though they scorned in their youth, they might wear in their age, and it was never too late to say *miserere*'.

[2] *The Art of English Poesy*, ed. Gladys D. Willcock and Alice Walker (Cambridge Univ., 1936), 303–4; cf. Frye 114. The gillyflower had two other relevant associations: it was a term for a loose woman (*OED* s.v. *Gillyflower* 2b, late examples only); and it was an emblem of gentleness (e.g. *A Handful of Pleasant Delights* (1584), ed. H. E. Rollins (New York: Dover, 1965), 5: 'Gillyflowers is for gentleness,/which in me shall remain:/Hoping that no sedition shall,/ Depart our hearts in twain.')

[3] Cf. Herrick's use of the Wisdom and Romans passages, *The Poetical Works of Robert Herrick*, ed. L. C. Martin (Oxford: Clarendon, 1968), 278, 'To His Friend, Master J. Jincks': 'The bastard slips may droop and die/Wanting both root, and earth; but thy/Immortal self, shall boldly trust. . . .'

creation ('an art that nature makes'), is in reality a splendid commonplace.[1] And although Polixenes seems put down, her immovable loyalty to simple original nature reaches a deeper spiritual level, where grace, not art, must amend. At the same time she represents in her own person an unsearchably complex grafting, in that she is intelligently innocent and simply or 'naturally' good. By nature royal, by nurture rustic, by festal art semi-divine, and by betrothal royal again, what is she when *by disguise* she becomes an African princess?[2] By contrast, Polixenes' behaviour represents a more confused, less satisfactory mixture. His disguise has an ulterior motive. And he seems to confuse Nature's bastards with those of human irregularity: valuing honour so excessively as to put it in effect above righteousness. His deficiency appears repeatedly: subtly in his suspicion that Florizel may not be 'gracious' (IV.ii.28), grossly in his tyrant's threat to torture Perdita. In fact, his scenes with Perdita and Florizel restate the theme of jealous rage, varied now by extension across the generation gap. (The analogy between Polixenes and Leontes is elaborate; extending to Camillo's similar ameliorations, and to such details as importunate jealous hospitality.)[3] It comes as a shock when gracefulness is attributed to Polixenes by the generously repentant Leontes (v.i.170).[4] Although he feels her attractiveness himself, Polixenes is an opponent of the simple, pure 'gracious' love that makes Perdita a blessing to her community.

Even the popular Autolycus, unexpectedly, is related to the same thematic complex. His suggestions are mythological—'My father named me Autolycus; who, being as I am, littered under Mercury, was likewise a snapper-up of unconsidered trifles' (IV.iii.24–6). Anciently, Autolycus was not merely an astrological 'child of Mercury' but Mercury's son. Shakespeare's Autolycus conforms to the mercurial archetype in his ingenious thefts, his

[1] Polixenes' grandiloquence, from the very start, is noted in M. M. Mahood, *'The Winter's Tale'* in Muir 214. On Polixenes as a Baconian improver, see Colie 275.

[2] Cf. *ibid.* 253 n. and 254; Bethell 93, 94; Nuttall 47–9 (on Perdita's civilized innocence).

[3] IV.ii.1–3; 10–20; cf. I.ii.1 ff.

[4] Cf. Mahood 228.

eloquence and his music (he sings five of the six songs solo, and leads in a sixth). Centuries before Mann's Felix Krull he is a representative of the cultural process; a parasitic improviser; a snapper-up, taking material from simple nature and exploiting the rustics with sophisticated and amoral arts—not least the tragi-comic art of the rogue-pastoral ballad.[1] Yet exploitation of nature is only a part of Autolycus' meaning. He is also a mercurial genius presiding over the many disguises of the last two acts. To say nothing of Autolycus' own Biblical disguise in search of a good Samaritan, Polixenes and Camillo disguise to spy; Perdita dresses up first as Flora, then in Autolycus' hat, an attribute of Mercury[2] that comes to her via Florizel, and finally as a Libyan princess; and Florizel becomes a shepherd, and then, by changing clothes with Autolycus, a ruined courtier. (Moreover, the metamorphoses of the Clown and the old Shepherd to gentlemen is strictly super-vised by Autolycus.) Mercury was also a god of deeper changes; so that the disguises (as often in Renaissance literature) externalize character transformation.[3] Perdita herself says: 'sure this robe of mine/Does change my disposition' (IV.iv.134–5). In part Autolycus contributes the spontaneous creativity of ordinary mundane social roles. But disguise has also a negative aspect, of deception; so that Florizel must set aside the Autolycus *persona*, and the in-stability of the Age of Mercury, before the action can reach its happy resolution.[4] Finally, in the concluding scene, the most pro-

---

[1] 'Doleful matter merrily set down', as the Clown says (IV.iv.190). See Taylor 333 for instances of boisterous pastoral.

[2] For Mercury's hat, see Jean Seznec, *The Survival of the Pagan Gods*, tr. Barbara F. Sessions, Bollingen Series 38 (New York: Pantheon, 1953), 211 etc.; Guy de Tervarent, *Attributs et symboles dans l'art profane 1450–1600*, Travaux d'humanisme et renaissance 29 (Geneva: Droz, 1958), col. 70.

[3] See Norman Holland, 'Disguise, Comic and Cosmic' in *The First Modern Comedies* (Cambridge, Mass.: Harvard, 1959), 45–63. On Marsilio Ficino's theory of Mercury's part in *conversio*, see Wind 123; on Mercury's relation to Flora, *ibid.* 126 n. Ficino's *In vita coelitus comparanda* III.5 discusses the neutral Mercury's moderating role in character formation. On Mercury as a god of mixture, see Ficino, *In Platonis Timaeum*, chs. XIX–XX.

[4] In the five-age as in the commoner (Ptolemaic) seven-age scheme, Mercury presided over the second age, *pueritia* (6–16 and 5–14 respectively): see Ptolemy, *Tetrabiblos*, IV.10 and consult Chew 163–9, Klibansky 149, n. 74, Franz Boll, 'Die Lebensalter', *Neue Jahrbücher für das klassische Altertum* 16 (1913), 89–154.

found transformation of all, the shedding of Hermione's disguise of stone, is achieved without Autolycus' arts.

The pastoral scenes, then, develop in metaphorical terms the 'hidden growth' that changes the character of Leontes. Far from being a mere interlude, they present symbols of the repair of nature; of the civilizing effect of art; of the gentling effect of time; of the interplay between nature and grace (as in Perdita's pageant of Flora); and of integration (as in the measurement of time, an emblem of temperance). Perdita's grace is not conceived as something super-added to nature, but as totally implicit; perfect mixture. Hence the placement of the Bohemian idyll: its natural phase allows time for grace to permeate and transform, edifying and growing a new nature. It is in the depths of ordinary goodness that the soul's life is to be recovered, it seems. Yet Bohemia is no 'merely' natural realm, but a mercurial place of mixture, where character transformation—under such common symbols as disguises and changing Ages—seems to happen all the time. And it is only after the Bohemian act that Cleomenes the oracle's messenger pronounces Leontes penitent: 'Sir, you have done enough' (v.i.1).

On Mercury's changeable influence, see Valeriano 358, on the five ages: assigning *pueritia* to Mercury, he continues: 'unde illud eius aetatis studium rerum plurimarum, et mutabilitas, et inconstantia, ut modo hoc, modo illud appetant . . .'

IV

How Old Was Leontes?

F. W. BATESON

WHAT'S in a number? Or—to vary Juliet's celebrated rhetorical question more precisely—what happens to an arithmetical unit when it enters into common speech as a word? Is *dozen* really synonymous with the figure 12—in spite of its ultimate derivation from the French *douze*? Why is it that 13 so immediately becomes 'unlucky' that some hotels' bedrooms jump from 12 to 14? The inherent disposition of figures to lose their mathematical purity in language is nicely illustrated by the idiom *to talk nineteen to the dozen*. The expression is immediately intelligible, but its memorability derives from the fact that it cannot be translated into a statistical description. It is almost a parody of an arithmetical process.

That Shakespeare was aware of the competing linguistic pulls of scientific precision and popular metaphor might be expected *a priori*. His plays are the verbal correlative of the intense contemporary battle in English society between the new sciences and the old superstitions. Simon Forman indeed, who saw one of the earliest performances of *The Winter's Tale* at the Globe, is rightly honoured as one of the heroic casualties of that battle: having discovered by astrology the day of his death he is believed to have committed suicide when the day arrived in order to fulfil his own prediction. In something of the same spirit John Hoskins wrote in his *Directions for Speech and Style* (c. 1599):

Whilst mathematics were in requests, all our similitudes came from lines, circles and angles; whilst moral philosophy is now a while spoken of, it is rudeness not to be sententious. And for my part I'll make one. I have used and outworn six several styles since I was first Fellow of New College, and am yet able to bear the fashion of the writing company.[1]

If Hoskins had outworn six styles since becoming (briefly) a Fellow of New College in 1586, that was only two a year. Shakespeare's styles changed at least once a year—and sometimes two or three times. And no one has doubted that he kept up with the writing company.

It was a stimulating time to be alive in, if also a dangerous time. The technique of survival may be said to have mainly depended upon the individual's appropriate behaviour within his particular social age-group. This is a topic Shakespeare has explored dramatically more fully in *The Winter's Tale* than in any of his other plays, and a new attitude in it to number-words, as it is best to call them, reflects the change stylistically.

A preliminary precaution will be to compare the use of these number-words with those in an earlier tragi-comedy. *Measure for Measure* suggests itself because it too is one of the mature plays that is not wholly successful. Both have puzzles, though *The Winter's Tale*'s principal puzzle—the apparently unmotivated behaviour of Leontes in the first two acts—is at any rate semi-soluble, or *perhaps* semi-soluble, by a numerical approach.

Measure for Measure has, on a rough count, some eighty number-words. (The count has to be rough because such words as *one* have other meanings, which have to be excluded, besides the numerical sense. The total of eighty includes each occurrence of the same number-word. The general criterion is that a figure can be substituted for the word without seriously disturbing the sense.) *The Winter's Tale*, which occupies three or four pages more in the 1623 Folio (from which both derive their *textus receptus*), has over a hundred number-words. Such common number-words as *half, one, two, three, four, five, six, seven* (with such variants as *once, first, twice, second,* etc.) occur with much the same frequency in both plays. Statistically, therefore, the two plays appear to be much of a muchness, considered arithmetically. It is only when the literary function of the number-words is asked that

[1] p. 39 of H. H. Hudson's edition of the MS (1935).

a striking difference shows up. In *Measure for Measure* the number-words tend to serve the plot; in *The Winter's Tale* they serve the theme, indeed almost embody the theme.

A third service the number-words supply is to add liveliness to what is being said by the rhetorical device of pseudo-specificity. Essentially in this context this is a figure of speech which exploits arithmetic for non-mathematical purposes. It is a literary equivalent of such colloquial idioms as *to talk nineteen to the dozen*, though the element of parody or 'nonsense' *à la* Lear or Carroll is less prominent in it. When the Second Gentleman in *Measure for Measure* refers to the 'three thousand dolours' the services of Mistress Overdone may have cost Lucio he is committing pseudo-specificity in its crudest form. (The 3000 is in competition with a pun—and loses.) Mistress Overdone's tribute to Claudio in the same scene (I.ii) is similar ('worth five thousand of you all'). Such grotesque overstatements—to which even the Duke succumbs in IV.i ('millions of false eyes')—have no arithmetical significance. The pull between what is said and what is meant is too great to be resolved in an effective Empsonian 'ambiguity'.

The numerical pseudo-specificity is of more interest when the figures employed are smaller and so have greater immediate human impact. Isabella, for example, suspecting that Claudio will after all decide that his own life is more worth preserving than his sister's chastity, 'quakes'

> Lest thou a feverous life shouldst entertain,
> And six or seven winters more respect
> Than a perpetual honour.

The six or seven winters do not have mathematical validity. Would not 5 or 6—*or* 7 or 8—have done as well? But, on the other hand, are they not perhaps the right ones here because the Elizabethan imagination is able to project itself into a future of 6/7 years distant, whereas 4/5 would be too few to be worth considering and 8/9 too many because too remote? But Isabella was certainly right to use number-words here rather than words without any human warmth to them such as *some* or *a few*.

Numerical pseudo-specificities do unquestionably enliven the conversation of Pompey and Lucio, but they do not assist either the progress of the plot or the development of the play's theme. Their effect is strictly local. Now, whereas most of the number-words in *Measure for Measure* are pseudo-specific and a fair few are plot-words (especially in Acts IV and V, where they accumulate as the 'fantastical duke of dark corners' shuffles the characters around), hardly any could be described as thematic. In *The Winter's Tale*, on the other hand, of the approximately hundred number-words some fifty are concerned with time—either directly in so many words (*hours, days, nights, weeks, months, years*), or in words implying a temporal sequence that cannot be accused of rhetoric (*first, once, two, twice, thrice*). The merely rhetorical use of number-words in *The Winter's Tale* is largely confined to the pseudo-specificities of the Clown and Autolycus (there are under forty altogether). And there are only six number-words solely necessitated by the plot.

I do not want to labour these statistics. What has most interested me in *The Winter's Tale* is the exceptional number of temporal references, no less than sixteen of them referring either directly or indirectly to the present age of the principal characters or their children. (The indirect reference is much the commonest.) Antigonus may inform us in so many words that he has three daughters: 'the eldest is eleven; the second and the third nine and some five' (II.i.144-5). But Antigonus—famous only for his exit 'pursued by a bear'—is a secondary character. The ages of Leontes, Polixenes, Mamillius, Perdita, and Florizel—the symbolic centres of the play—have to be worked out arithmetically from clues in the number-words. This is not nearly as easy as the sums presented by the First Grave-Digger to his colleague in *Hamlet*, from which we learn that the Prince of Denmark is thirty years old; but a correct answer is a great deal more important if we are to respond critically.

The entrance of Time as 'the Chorus' is significantly at the mid-point of the play. By sliding 'O'er sixteen years' (IV.i.6), Time makes it clear that Perdita is now sixteen, the age confirmed in Paulina and Camillo's remarks (V.iii.31,50) about the sixteen years that had passed since Act III. It is true Camillo—or the

copyist or printer responsible for IV.ii.4—tells Polixenes that 'It is
fifteen years since I saw my country'. But the discrepancy is im-
material, and only the fussiest editor would now emend fifteen
in this passage to sixteen, as Hanmer and Capell found it necessary to do in the eighteenth century. The number-word's appearance here is to prepare the way for Perdita whose age is easily
inferred from it. Perdita is now at the age when, according to
medieval and Renaissance symbolic convention, feminine beauty
reached its peak. (It was fifteen or sixteen or thereabouts; in the
passage about his three daughters already referred to Antigonus
seems to reduce it to fourteen.)

Perdita, then, in the loose unarithmetical sense of dramatic
speech is, as her age presumes, pre-eminently beautiful, her girlish
freshness unravaged by small-pox or the cares of the world.
Florizel, her masculine equivalent and natural mate, is corres-
pondingly twenty-one or thereabouts. Leontes's first comment
when they meet is spontaneous and convincing:

> Were I but twenty-one,
> Your father's image is so hit in you,
> His very air, that I should call you brother,
> As I did him ...
>
> (v.i.125-7)

So we now know too, as indeed had already been made clear in
the image of 'twinn'd lambs' in the second scene of the play (I.ii.
66), that Leontes and Polixenes were the same age. But what was
that? Here a literary detective may be required. In the same dramatic, almost melodramatic, second scene Leontes, in the agony
of an unmotivated conviction of Hermione's infidelity, explains
away his 'brow of much distraction' by saying

> Looking on the lines
> Of my boy's face, methoughts I did recoil
> Twenty-three years, and saw myself unbreech'd ...
>
> (I.ii.153-5)

The 23 years are oddly, provocatively, precise. 23 is also as it
happens, the number of days, as Leontes himself notes (II.iii.197),

that Cleomenes and Dion take to obtain the Delphic oracle's pro-
nouncement and return to Sicily with it. Later the first thing the
Shepherd says, his entry-line, is 'I would there were no age
between ten and three-and-twenty . . . for there is nothing in the
between but getting wenches with child, wronging the ancientry,
stealing, fighting' (III.iii.59–60). There is no obvious connection
between the three passages, but they may help to keep its first use
fresh in the audience's mind.

With the clue that Leontes is only twenty-three years older than
the child Mamillius then was, all that remains to be discovered is
Mamillius's age in I.ii. Well, Mamillius is almost exactly the same
age as Florizel according to Paulina ('There was not full a month/
Between their births', v.i.117–18). And, as Florizel is some five, or
just possibly six, years older than Perdita, Leontes must be 5
(6?)+23=28 (possibly 29) years old in Acts I and II. And, of
course, 44 (possibly 45) in Acts IV and V.

With the ages of the principal characters established,[1] it is
possible to be more precise about the nature of Leontes's jealousy
and the necessary length of his period of penitence. The evidence
is available in the episode within the sheep-sharing feast scene, in
which Perdita distributes or assigns flowers to the guests appropriate to their respective ages. She begins with Polixenes and Camillo,
who are disguised—clearly as old men—and receive 'flowers of
winter (rosemary and rue). Winter is preceded by autumn[2] ('the
year growing ancient,/Not yet on summer's death nor on the
birth/Of trembling winter'), but Perdita has no flowers for guests
in the autumn of their lives, because carnations and gilly-flowers
(pinks) that flower in August and September can be streaked
artificially—a process of which she disapproves and the disguised
Polixenes defends in a memorable passage. Those shepherds who

[1] Except Hermione's. But Hermione, a variant spelling of Harmonia in
classical mythology and pronounced HARMIONE in the early seventeenth century,
is ageless, almost supernatural, reappearing from the tomb like Alcestis. Her
role is to bring harmony into the play. As she lacks an opposite number,
Polixenes's wife having apparently died (she is never mentioned), her age need
not be counted in human years.

[2] Perdita avoids the word. It was used less frequently than *spring*, *summer* and
winter in Shakespeare's time.

are 'men of middle age' are then given 'flowers/Of middle summer' ('hot' lavender, mint, savory, marjoram, marigolds). The
'flowers o' th' spring' (lilies of the valley, daffodils, violets, primroses, etc.) 'that might/Become your time of day' would have been
given to Florizel and the young shepherdesses if such flowers had
been available. (The shearing feast takes place in summer.)

This bald summary of iv.iv.73–127 has been needed to demon-
strate that Perdita is using flowers in this episode to illustrate with
rural exactitude the Four Ages of Man, a Renaissance commonplace even more popular then than the classical Seven Ages of
Man that Jaques played with in *As You Like It* (ii.vii.143 ff.).
Jaques's catalogue however has a purely local and personal significance. It is irrelevant either to plot or theme. But Perdita's
flowers have a direct reference to the theme of *The Winter's Tale*
—perhaps even to Shakespeare himself.

The link between the Four Ages of Man and the temporal
core of the play is the age of the principal characters in Acts
i to iii on the one hand and iv and v on the other. A diagram which
gives the modern reader a painless bird's-eye-view of what the
Four Ages must have meant to an Elizabethan playgoer is provided in Thomas Walkington's *The Optick Glasse of Humors*
(1607). *Adolescentia*, the spring of human life (*Ver*), is 'Sanguine'
(blood is the dominant humour); man's summer (*Aestas*) is
Juventus, which is 'Choleric'; his Autumnus is *Vergens Aetas*
(the stooping age), which is 'Phlegmatic'; finally *Senectus* is
man's *Hyems* (winter), which is 'Melancholic'. Walkington's
diagram, which has been reproduced by Lawrence Babb in
Elizabethan Melancholy (East Lansing, 1951, p. 11), also gives the
four winds identifiable with the Four Ages, the characteristic
elements (air for *Adolescentia*, fire for *Juventus*, water for middle
age, earth for old age), the dominant planets (Jupiter, Mars, the
moon, Saturn in the same seasonal order), and finally the all-
determining sign of the zodiac (*Libra*, the Scales, for *Adolescentia*;
Leo, the lion, for *Juventus*; Virgo, the virgin, for middle age;
Scorpio, the scorpion, for old age).

That Shakespeare *believed* in this elaborate quadripartite division
of physical reality seems unlikely, but that he was prepared to *use*

it as a traditional store-house of symbols or metaphors is certain. Cleopatra describes herself as 'all air and fire' as she dies, having shed her 'baser elements' (water and earth). Ariel too is no doubt intended to incarnate air and fire, with water and earth represented by Caliban. *The Winter's Tale*, however, uses the conventional framework much more elaborately and consistently. The modern reader who insists on applying A. C. Bradley's canons of psychological realism to the exclusion of symbolic factors is certainly misreading the play. On the other hand, such symbolic interpretations as those of Wilson Knight and Traversi, which depend exclusively on the internal evidence of imagery, are incomplete because they neglect the numerical patterns or traditional concepts that would have been familiar to Shakespeare and his original audience.

Walkington omitted from his diagram the precise ages, defined in years, at which *Adolescentia, Juventus, Vergens Aetas* and *Senectus* begin and end. There was little agreement about this in either the Four Ages or the Seven Ages scheme. Shakespeare must have known the formulas in Sir Thomas Elyot's immensely popular *The Castle of Health* (first edition 1534) and the age-divisions in *The Winter's Tale* agree fairly well with Elyot's ages, excluding childhood (a period, as E. E. Kellett once pointed out, in which Shakespeare shows curiously little interest). They are best tabulated:

'Adolescency'   15–25 ('Cupid and Venus very busy')
'Juventute'   25–39 ('reign of the humor named Coler')
'Old Age'   40–60
'Senectute'   After 60

If Perdita has been sixteen years in Bohemia by Acts IV and V she has certainly reached 'Adolescency' (only just if she is fifteen). Both she and Florizel are therefore entitled to keep 'Cupid and Venus very busy'. That Leontes might have become choleric when he was twenty-five is certainly possible. His name suggests that he was born under the zodiacal sign Leo, whose planet was Mars. A rival formula[1] to Elyot's specifies twenty-eight as the age

[1] See Philippe Aries, *Centuries of Childhood* (English version, Penguin Books, 1962), 19.

when *Juventus* begins. Had Shakespeare's copy been of one of the later editions of *The Castel of Health* that changed twenty-five to twenty-eight? The sudden savage irruption of jealousy could then be attributable to an exchange of dominant humours at that age, blood in excess becoming choler in excess. In any case the fact that he was forty-four (or forty-five) in Acts IV and V and therefore automatically 'Phlegmatic' would justify Paulina in restoring Hermione to him. There will be no more 'Choleric' explosions now.

A final speculation may be ventured. It is still generally agreed —even by those hard-faced academics who have done very well out of Shakespeare—that an indirect autobiographical allusion was intended in Prospero's abjuring his 'rough magic' in the last scene of *The Tempest*. If, as seems certain, *The Winter's Tale* was first performed in either the autumn of 1610 or early in 1611 it must have been written in 1609/1610, probably at Stratford. Shakespeare celebrated his forty-fifth birthday in April 1609. Leontes was forty-four (possibly, if Camillo's memory can be trusted in IV.ii, forty-five). Perhaps the coincidence may be allowed to suggest some autobiographical basis to the play.[1] A poet's number-words need not in any case be arithmetically precise, need they?

Postscript

My friend Alastair Fowler, who (if I may be excused the pseudo-specificity) is at least a *hundred* times more learned than I am in the Renaissance's numerological fantasies, assures me that Shakespeare is more likely to have adopted an Ages of Man scheme that is found in Valeriano, the author of *Hieroglyphica*, than from Sir Thomas Elyot. I agree that 45, the age at which Valeriano's *juniores* turn into *seniores*, is in closer agreement with my own conclusion that Leontes is 44 in Acts IV and V. And my demonstration (if I may be allowed to call it that) that Leontes is 28 in Acts

---

[1] The comparative success of psycho-analytic interpretations of Leontes's jealousy may be thought to confirm an autobiographical element. See the persuasive essay on Leontes by Murray M. Schwartz in *The Practice of Psychoanalytic Criticism* (ed. Leonard Tennenhouse, Detroit, 1976), 202–25.

I to III is nearer 30, when *adolescentes* become *juniores* according to Valeriano, than the 25 Elyot allotted to the change from 'Adolescencie' to 'Juventute'.

Clearly, however, both Valeriano and Elyot preferred to stick to round figures whenever possible. Shakespeare was much more specific—because, I have suggested, he was being autobiographical. If 44 can mean in his forty-fourth year, then Leontes's emergence from penitential seclusion has its biographical parallel—though not of course necessarily an equation—with the period when the Last Plays began (1608). And Leontes's age in Acts I to III must equally suggest a real turning-point in the young Shakespeare's life (1564+28=1592) and temperament of which the literary manifestations were *Venus and Adonis* and the earliest of the *Sonnets*. A Summer's Tale, in fact.

I have one card up my sleeve of which Professor Fowler may be unaware. This is the autobiography of the madrigalist Thomas Whythorne (not published until 1962). As his editors point out Whythorne, born in 1528 and writing in 1576, saw his own past life as conforming to Elyot's formula in the *Castel of Helth*:

> I had then learned that, after the age of childhood (which continueth from the infancy until fifteen) beginneth the age named adolescency, which continueth until twenty and five. This said age is the first part of the young man's age ... (p.18)
> ... as the blood reigneth chiefly in the juventute, the which is from the twenty-fifth until forty years of age, which is called the second and last part of the young man's age; so the humour named choler doth chiefly reign in the second and last part of the young man's age (p. 66)
> And therefore I considering with myself that I was now above thirty years of age and growing toward the age of forty, at which years begins the first part of the old man's age ... (p. 117).

Why then did Shakespeare call the play *The Winter's Tale* (not *A* but *The*)? Because, ultimately, he wanted to confront dramatically the arrival of his own old man's age.

F. W. B.

V

Froude's Revenge, or the Carlyles and Erasmus A. Darwin

K. J. FIELDING

'HISTORY is the essence of innumerable Biographies',[1] biography is
made up of details, and for those long dead the details come from
documents. It is the inescapable truth for any editor of letters, and
in pursuing those of the Carlyles I was led to look at the letters of
the Wedgwood family. It turns out that close as their friendship
was with Carlyle, it must have been much less—and less interesting—than what they tell of the friendship of the Carlyles and
Erasmus Darwin.[2]

There are a number of reasons for wanting to know more about
their association, obscure as Darwin has become. In the first place
it is one we know *of* but little about. In the second, Erasmus has an

---

[1] Carlyle, 'On History', *Works*, XXVII (London, Centenary edn., 1899), 86.

[2] Erasmus Alvey Darwin (1804–81), hereafter ED, has to be identified as
Charles Darwin's elder brother, and grandson of Erasmus Darwin (1731–1802),
author of *The Loves of the Plants* (1789), *Zoonamia* (1796), etc. ED's father was
Dr Robert Darwin (1766–1848), who married Susannah Wedgwood, daughter
of the potter, Joseph of Etruria (1730–95) and sister of Josiah of Etruria and Maer
(1769–1843). He qualified as Bachelor of Medicine, but weak health and
sufficient means led him to choose a life of leisure. For a valuable account and
excerpts from about a dozen of his letters see Grace Calder, 'Erasmus A. Darwin,
Friend of Thomas and Jane Carlyle', *MLQ*, 20 (1959), 36–48, hereafter GC. Her
texts came only from some family copies, but all ED's letters quoted here (unless otherwise noted) are from MSS, Josiah Wedgwood & Sons Ltd, Barlaston,
Stoke-on-Trent, and the University Library, Keele, to whom I am grateful for
permission to examine and publish from them. ED is frequently referred to in
Emma Darwin, A Century of Family Letters, 1792–1896, ed. by her daughter
Henrietta Litchfield, 2 vols. (London, 1915), hereafter Litchfield, which was
based on the same Wedgwood papers; but for the sake of brevity I have tried
to avoid using previously printed texts. For the help of Dr Ian Fraser, Archivist
at Keele, I am much more than conventionally indebted, and I am grateful to
Mr Francis Doherty.

attractiveness strongly felt by all who knew him. Thirdly, though wispy and elusive, his friendship with the Carlyles has a special quality which may enlighten us about them, for we have often heard so much about the curmudgeonliness of Carlyle that it must come as a surprise to many that he was not only tolerated but loved and sought after by the very men who might have been expected to detest him. For here is a friend who remained attached to Carlyle for over forty years, who was liberal, sceptical, notably gentle in manners, and who certainly cared nothing for his doctrine of Work, but who probably shared the affections of the Carlyles more continuously than anyone else.

Yet, because of the accidents that beset letters, those on both sides were almost entirely lost, and the story of their friendship vanished. Piecing it together again from other family letters, in the main unpublished, half-dated, misdated and undated altogether, is difficult. But what justifies it is that as the story emerges it shows not only a peculiarly interesting minor figure on the fringes of Victorian literary and intellectual society, but Carlyle himself in a new light. The standard, four-volume biography by Froude has long been notoriously unsatisfactory: for Froude was self-opinionated, independent, and at odds with so many of Carlyle's surviving friends, that his account has always left the sense of something missing. As G. B. Tennyson says, 'It is not only the excessive dwelling on Jane's alleged sorrows or on Carlyle's acerbity or even the exasperating use of documents; it is a certain heaviness, even a gloom (as Froude said of Carlyle, "Gloom clung to him like a shadow").'[1] For it was only about 1860 that Froude became intimate with Carlyle as he was entering a period of seeming 'weak, passionate, complaining . . . lonely, irritable and morbid' (*Life*, IV, 458); and his whole account of Carlyle's life is darkened by looking backward from the shadows of old age.

Even this might not have mattered if his study of Carlyle had been purely biographical, and less obviously more able than those of his rivals. But, even in his own day, men and women had got

[1] 'The Carlyles', in *Victorian Prose, A Guide to Research*, ed. David J. DeLaura (New York, Modern Language Association, 1973), 46–7.

used to seeing Carlyle as representative of his age, and Carlyle himself was inclined to cast himself as a 'prophet'. So that, what we have so long been given as an 'official' view, has been the tale of Carlyle projected as a typical Victorian, recounted as if he were perpetually as sour as he sometimes seems to have been in Froude's company, and told by someone who never knew at first hand the issues that roused him in his prime.

That there is something to be said for Froude cannot be denied. But *he* has said it all. It is what he did *not* say but excluded that may now concern us. For an earlier Carlyle is rediscoverable: someone much more human, and more truly representative of his age and best work. It is this which I hope an account of the friendship of the Carlyles and Erasmus Darwin will help to show, leading up to the realization that this was deliberately suppressed by Froude who was upset at the attacks made on him by some of the old Cheyne Row associates just as he had begun the *Life*.

There may be other general conclusions that could be drawn: that this is often the condition of biography, that in his very nature the 'official biographer' is often someone as deeply concerned about his own opinions as those of the person he is writing about, that our understanding of a period depends on biographical readings and that such readings depend on what we know about those writing them. But there is no escape from details and documents. It is where it begins and ends, as in the story of this friendship.

It begins by being a striking example of how, soon after Carlyle's arrival in London, his attraction was largely for liberals and radicals, or men whose opinions seem quite unlike his own. We find them not just in the group round John Stuart Mill, or Carlyle's former student the radical M.P., Charles Buller, or the French St-Simonians, or literary friends such as Leigh Hunt, but it is remarkable how Carlyle could maintain animated and polite conversation not only with extremists such as the revolutionary Godefroy Cavaignac, 'the intensest of athiests',[1] but could happily

---

[1] J. S. Mill to Carlyle, 25 Nov. 1833: see F. W. Hilles, 'The Hero as Revolutionary: Godefroy Cavaignac', *Carlyle and His Contemporaries, Essays in Honor of Charles Richard Sanders*, ed. John Clubbe (Durham, N.C., 1976), 77.

bring him together with men such as the saintly Thomas Erskine of Linlathen, the firmest and most theologically minded of conservatives.[1] Strange as it may seem, there was a certain sanity about Carlyle that made it possible for him to bring together men who were completely opposed.

Erasmus introduced himself to the Carlyles in May 1835, when he contrived to call on them 'very ingeniously'. From the first he was attracted to Jane, 'a divine little woman . . . who came and seated herself behind me. . . . She kept up one unceasing chatter about Craigenputtoch and everything else in the world.' Carlyle was uncharacteristically talked down by Erasmus's companion, but distinguished himself by arriving in 'a green hat the size of a small umbrella. . . . It is absurd after going to see him', wrote Erasmus, 'but I really don't think I should be able to recognize him in the street if he should not have his green hat on.'[2]

For a while the record is faint, but the friendship grew stronger through the association of the Carlyles with the Wedgwoods and their circle of 'Saints' including Thomas Erskine and the Rev. Alexander Scott. Carlyle wrote about them to his family early in 1837 to say that Fanny Wedgwood was 'really a very nice little woman'. Others in their circle were Harriet Martineau, whom they had known since 1833, and Erasmus, 'who has been hovering about this good while, and of late (thro *Martineau*dom &c) has

---

[1] Thomas Erskine (1788–1870) of Linlathen, theologian and advocate, was a family connection of the Wedgwoods, who became a great friend of Carlyle's. He was a liberal churchman (a friend of F. D. Maurice), something of an Irvingite, and a conservative with a strong concern for the poor. Julia Wedgwood was to write to him as 'breaking through the hard Calvinism then thought orthodoxy', and that 'his life recurs to one's memory like the sigh of an exile': see her *Nineteenth Century Teachers* (London, 1909).

[2] To Frances (Fanny) Wedgwood, dated ?1836–7 by GC, but certainly late May 1835. From MS, Wedgwood papers: all otherwise unascribed quotations are from these letters of ED to Fanny, which are not distinguished except by date, and other unascribed letters are also from the Wedgwood papers. In all there are about 200 letters from ED to Frances Wedgwood, her husband Hensleigh and family. Frances Wedgwood (1800–89) was daughter of Sir James Mackintosh, and married in 1832. Hensleigh (1803–91), grandson of Josiah Wedgwood of Etruria and son of Josiah of Etruria and Maer, was thus first cousin of Erasmus and Charles Darwin. Appointed a paid police magistrate in 1831, he amazed and impressed his family, late in 1837, by resigning over a question of conscience about administering oaths.

been brought nearer: a tall, bashful, sensibilish most good-natured man . . . who does nothing but read a little, be "the cousin of everybody" and drive a cab!' The Wedgwoods, said Carlyle, 'seem determined to cultivate us', and Erasmus had persuaded Jane to introduce him to F. D. Maurice, and altogether 'it seems a strange fluctuating thing your circle of society here'.[1]

It is of some interest to see that though the Wedgwoods might be thought better off for interesting society than the Carlyles, it was they who made the first approaches. There is no doubt that the Carlyles were a powerful attraction to those who wanted fresh ideas and pleasant company. For a long while they took a central position in this whole group, a fact which deserves attention in itself. But as far as Erasmus and the Wedgwoods were concerned, their interest in the Carlyles lay primarily in their cultivated and intelligent talk, much of it free and witty as well as well-informed, polemical, entirely independent, and still fundamentally inspired by the strong spirit of public concern that moved others in the circle. In an age of frequently servile public conformity, they admired the Carlyles' sincerity, conviction and good humour. On their own part, the tone of the Wedgwood and Darwin family letters resembles that of the best families of Jane Austen's novels, which they particularly admired, being well aware of the likeness themselves. It consisted of a combination of graciousness, intellect, mutual affection and high principle, which they also recognized in the self-cultivation of the Carlyles, who were not opposites but kindred spirits.

If this seems a paradox it is because we have previously been misinformed. It is true that in any association with Thomas, lay the possibility of his shattering decorum with rhetorical bombshells. Yet this gave an added zest, and was his second main attraction. For the decorum of the Darwins and Wedgwoods lay under a tense restraint which they sometimes needed to relieve by admiration for an out-spoken hero, though always ready to

---

[1] To Dr John Carlyle, 17 Feb., MS:NLS, 523.45; a year later Carlyle wrote to John about them all again (1 Feb. 1838): 'Erasmus Darwin, a grandson of the great Darwin . . . comes often here,—driving his cab . . . a very polite, good, quiet man.'

retreat for security within the walls of convention. Erasmus himself had sufficient independence of means and character to need no vent beyond mild sarcastic wit; but Fanny, as well as some of her more outspoken aunts, often felt herself an open 'radical', and in this lay part of the excitement of her newfound friendship.

There is a problem in dealing with the evidence of their association that the new material is too abundant for those who like transcripts at length and *verbatim*, and to those who don't it may seem small beer. Yet without being too selective my main aim is to see what Erasmus was like and the nature of their friendship.

While it was fresh, Erasmus writes (27 Dec. 1837) as if news of the Carlyles were all important:

I spent the livelong day at Chelsea on Monday, having received orders to that effect to come & help them be miserable and tho' we did not effect that we certainly contrived to be gently dull. If it had been the least bit colder we should however have been effectually miserable as they had no coals in the house & being Xmas day could buy none, so that Thomas and I had to relieve one another constantly at the bellows to keep up the least spark of fire. . . . I think you would have felt flattered if you could have heard how very nicely poor Thomas spoke of you & his visit to Clapham on Sunday, all the speculations he made about you, and all the things he saw which certainly required his dreaming eyes to see, and how when Jenny [Jane Carlyle] contrived to edge in her little word, he very properly snubbed her for supposing you to be quite perfect, and not content with thieves carrying off all your goods was inclined to inflict all manner of misfortunes upon [you] as everything at last was sure to turn out for your own good. [The Wedgwoods had just been burgled.] I several times had to keep the peace between them as much as I would between Sno & Bro [the Wedgwoods' children]. He got upon the inevitable subject of slavery in spite of repeated threats of Harriet, and seeing no chance of the beautiful relations of master & slave being reestablished in Europe, he got quite pathetic over himself in the impossibility of his having 'a little black boy' which he seemed to think would cure all his domestic evils, there being then a new maid servant in the house no doubt a great aggravation. The histories which Lady Jeffry gave him of the way in which her slaves were treated & the love more than that of a family seems to have been the original of all his hallucinations on this subject.[1] He called upon me next day & is coming again on Friday.

There were more 'homeopathic doses of news'. The next letter (10–11 Jan. 1838) chronicles how Erasmus had been 'nurse' to 'Thomas', and what a hard time he had 'to make him come'. But when he did, he began to be enraptured with one of the Erskine brothers:

This morning, out of mere tedium vitae I went thro' a snow storm to Chelsea to try if their company was more amusing than my own, and this evening he came to me from the same sort of feeling I suppose, & tomorrow we [are] going to Mrs Rich in the vain hope of bullying her out of some books which Mr Scott carried away . . . & after that to call upon our love Mr Erskine if he has not left town.

He is amused by parodies of Carlyle's style in the *Times*, which Carlyle received with 'Homeric peals of laughter', wrongly assigning them to Thackeray.[2] The same letter ends:

I do nothing but meditate deeply over the fire, & have a suspicion that I am getting uncommonly fat, but as I know that I am very stupid I proposed to Jenny that we should write a joint stock letter, the only answer to which was a prodigiously long shake of the head, which meant I suppose that there would not be even a flap left vacant in one of the endless epistles she is going to send you.

Almost immediately the new friends made themselves useful, and led by Harriet Martineau they supported the first series of Carlyle's lectures in May 1837. There were to be four in all, ending in 1840. All practical arrangements were undertaken for

[1] Anti-slavery was innate in a Darwin or Wedgwood, and Harriet Martineau was already a renowned abolitionist. Lord Jeffrey had married a Miss Wilkes from Philadelphia.
[2] By Disraeli: see *Whigs and Whiggism*, ed. W. Hutcheon (London, 1913), 408.

him, Hensleigh lent him a rare book to flourish at the audience, and Erasmus escorted Fanny. 'We were agreeably surprised', she reported, 'to see the room very decently full & a very good audience . . . & Eras says Mr C. talks of making £150 by these lectures which we all thought wd have been such a failure'.[1] Three weeks later she has to say that William Empson thought them 'not highly rated' and that Carlyle 'does not take pains enough, they are certainly much inferior to his conversation'. But she had made 'great friends' with Jane, whom Erasmus's sisters had enjoyed visiting, though it was 'a great piece of duty their going to Carlyles 2 last lectures & paying their guineas to please Erasmus'.[2]

The time of preparation for lectures, which were given without notes, was always one of strain. On 5 April 1838, Erasmus writes:

> Poor Thomas has come & smoked his pipe pretty often with me this week getting his syllabus ready. . . . I tremble when I think of it. . . . I witnessed this morning a most rapturous meeting between little Jeffery & Jenny. He kept patting & coaxing her as you would a little dog—it was rather pretty.

When the lectures were over, Thomas took a holiday in Scotland, and Erasmus continued to call on Jane:

> It has so happened for my sins that when I have ventured there of an evening I have had to talk broken french or Italian, with the exception of one evening when there was a grand Scott party, and some Irvingites to meet them. It was the most awful looking circle of females I ever profaned.
>
> (2 Sep. 1838)

Yet Jane did not please everyone. Harriet Martineau clearly found it hard to like her. Fanny Wedgwood was enthusiastic at first and always warmly affectionate. But when Erasmus brought his brother Charles, in May 1838, he could not feel in the least the same. 'Jenny', he wrote to Emma Wedgwood his *fiancée*, 'sent some civil messages to you, but which, from the effects of a

[1] To her sister-in-law Sarah Elizabeth Wedgwood, 3 May.
[2] To same, 27 May.

hysterical sort of giggle, were not very intelligible. It is high treason, but I cannot think' her 'either quite natural or lady-like', but 'one must always like Thomas'. Charles was to continue meeting Carlyle from time to time, as with Erasmus in January 1839, when he thought him 'in high force. . . . To my mind Carlyle is the best worth listening to of any man I know'. The Wedgwoods had been present also, and 'such society', Charles found 'worth all other and more brilliant kinds many times over'.[1]

In 1839 Harriet Martineau retired to Tynemouth, near Newcastle, and made rather desperate efforts to keep the group together. In July 1841 she wrote to Jane reporting on a solo holiday-visit from Carlyle, full of enthusiasm that 'Eras: is really coming; & you probably,—and Mrs Wedgwood possibly. Hurra!' She doubted 'whether so merry a person', as Thomas, 'has been in my parlour'.[2] But Jane held back, comforted by visits by Erasmus, whom she called 'the likest thing to a brother I ever had in the world';[3] and when she went north it was to a miserable cottage-holiday with Thomas at Newby, near Annan, finished off by a return to London just calling on Harriet. Erasmus made the journey on his own, moderately enjoying it. But it was not all harmony. Clearly Fanny had even less wish to drag herself up to the north-east with or without her family, and Erasmus writes:

> As for Tynemouth that will require a great deal of considera-tion. . . . I suppose it is Mrs Jenny's doing, who looks forward to making poor Thomas by that time sufficiently uncomfortable at Annan to move his quarters. Does not the downright radi-calism in her letter rather startle you. One can hear the same things said ironically to shew one's disgust at things in general and only so—wishing for a famine and the like.

The fact is that Carlyle's difficulties in writing *Cromwell* were making themselves felt while he was unable to make headway.

[1] Litchfield, II.13 and 21.
[2] Harriet to Jane, early summer, and 4 July 1841, MS:NLS, 2883, 94–7, and 104.
[3] Jane to Mary Scot, Spring 1841, quoted by L. and E. Hanson, *Necessary Evil* (London, 1952), 259.

Yet, throughout the forties, the friendship remains extremely active, and without chronicling every letter their quality is interesting. Jane confidingly shows Erasmus a manuscript essay on Carlyle lent her by Mazzini ('the little murderer') who had asked her to advise him on 'whether it . . . would hurt Carlyle's feelings'. Thomas shows him a letter from Jeffrey, 'full of abuse of Past & Present. The affectation, the masses of rubbish—were some of the mild terms he used. . . . In short it was the letter of a friend.' They visit the Elgin marbles together, 'pass a very pleasant frosty evening together with nothing very memorable', or just meet without there being 'a particle of Chelsea news that I know of to tell you' (7 Aug. 1842). The record is so incomplete because the Wedgwoods are also writing and calling on the Carlyles themselves. He was notoriously not the easiest person to get to dine out, but for Fanny, Erasmus suggests, it just might be possible. While Carlyle takes a summer holiday in 1843, Darwin keeps an eye on Jane, calling after dinner and remarking 'that I "looked as if I needed to go to Gunter's and have an ice"', or driving her out, and uttering 'sarcastic things . . . in good Darwin style'.[1] Next year he kept Carlyle company while she was away; and on her return was called on in emergency.

Jane had discovered that a German friend named Plattnauer had been arrested and taken to an insane asylum. It was, of course, Erasmus whose cab allowed him the privilege of driving her to see what had happened:

> I took her there crying with agitation expecting to find him chained in a dungeon, & then came crying back with the pleas-ure of finding it such a nice place & such a nice set of people who assured her he would soon be well. The poor man has gone and established himself with your friend Mr Grieves at Ham Common & after a few days he declared they did not carry out their principles & so to illustrate them he came down to his work stark naked & then broke all the windows—then to prison & so to the Asylum.
>
> (13 Aug. 1844)

[1] *Letters and Memorials* (London, 1883), I, 237 and 255, Jane to Thomas, 18 and 28 Aug.

As soon as he was 'cured' the Carlyles asked him to stay with them.

A German governess, Amelie Bölte, was another *protegée*: at least, she seems to be the 'German poetess', Erasmus refers to as 'an enchanting little woman' who

> made really quite beautiful poetry in an instant, & spoke so clearly it was a pleasure to listen to her. The poor little soul was in some trouble, & when she went away they found they had not got her address & Thomas actually came up with me to hunt her out so I think his stony heart was rather touched.
>
> (20 Aug. 1843?)

Altogether throughout these years this friendship gives us the impression of a much livelier Carlyle than Froude's aged companion; and this is so even though Erasmus himself was sometimes an invalid, and an aunt could write (4 May 1845), 'I was very much shocked to see Erasmus—if he does not get better soon I should fear his case was hopeless'.[1] There was to be an alarming illness in 1854, but he was never entirely subdued during Carlyle's lifetime.

Although it is impossible to give all the extracts, it is easy to convey the sense of them. Early in the New Year 1848, Jane writes to Thomas that Darwin called with another friend while she was in bed with a cold, and they went away; but that Darwin then called again, 'and this time I had him up—very *quiet* and kind'.[2] On 1 May, Erasmus writes, 'I have rashly exposed myself to a transcendentalist dinner at Chelsea', probably in Emerson's honour; and, about the same time, 'Thomas came yesterday having been outtalked by Macaulay to revenge himself on me'.

Erasmus is in and out of Cheyne Row in the early fifties, not just sustaining Jane, but for the pleasure of Thomas's company. On 29 December 1850, Carlyle records in his journal that Erasmus and Charles Kingsley came to dinner, and on 30 January Erasmus writes, 'I am going to a tipsy party on Wednesday and on Thursday with Chelsea . . . to a model prison at Pentonville', and

---

[1] Fanny Allen to Elizabeth Wedgwood.
[2] MS:NLS, 604.260.

explains that he had just dined at Chelsea with the poet Henry
Taylor, who had made some cryptic remark about the clergy,
adding ironically: 'I think both Carlyle and I felt that we had fallen
in with an esprit fort'.

There are reasons for thinking that Erasmus enjoyed the role of
inoffensive sceptic, in religion as in nearly everything else,[1] and
this may have given a relish to Carlyle's occasional outbursts
against the Church. The preparations for the *Latter-Day Pamphlets*
(including the Pentonville visit) were another matter. The Wedgwoods had responded to the spirit of 1848 and were possibly
growing tired of Carlyle's growling reaction, although friendly
relations continued. Erasmus tried to tolerate it, but about February 1850 he writes:

> I saw Thomas yesterday very miserable in the pangs of labour
> beginning to print a series of pamphlets occasional discourses
> beneficent whips or whatever the title is. I feel rather alarmed,
> as one can't stand a great deal of such stuff.

It is perhaps a year or two before this that he refers to Mill's
criticism of Carlyle's articles on Ireland in the *Spectator* in 1848:

> I found he had read Mill but so that what was not self-evident
> to him he has 'ghastly phantasm' & seemed quite perplexed
> why people on every side would bring forward these phan-
> tasms against his regimented labour.

About 1847 he noted,

> Carlyle's ferocity is like a child's so that really one hardly cares
> for it more than Tim's, [the youngest Wedgwood's], unfor-
> tunately he has no Ma to carry him off cursing and swearing
> as some beloved angels sometimes do.

[1] Emma Darwin wrote to Charles early in their married life about his own
scepticism, which distressed her, suggesting that it may have partly come from
Erasmus, 'whose understanding you have such a very high opinion of, and for
whom you have so much affection'. (Litchfield, II, 173).

Yet Carlyle's friends stood it and, with the exception of listening to him on the negro question, perhaps even enjoyed it. It was the Wedgwood belief that the kind of allowances that have to be made for anyone with toothache had to be allowed Carlyle at any time. Yet, though they must have deplored the spirit in which Carlyle turned to the history of *Frederick*, Fanny sent a bust of his hero to inspire him, and Erasmus noted (possibly after the first two volumes in 1858), 'The old grey beard came and smoked the pipe of tranquillity and brought me his Prinzenraub which I haven't had the heart to begin yet'.

Many of Erasmus's letters turn on whether or not Carlyle could be aroused to perform. In 1846 he is delighted when Thomas Spedding provokes him to a furious outburst, and then urges him 'to write his theory of Religion to show what a mass of inconsistencies he is composed of'. But, another time, he only reports that he 'found Thomas asleep in which state he remained morally most of the evening' (2 Sep. ?1850). Or again:

A sober evening, and some old enthusiast came with a spiritual system of physiology & rather crossified Carlyle. Mrs. Jenny had an amusing account of an awful discussion that he & Macaulay got into which Lady [Ashburton] contrived to stop, and after dinner Lord A told Jenny that they were worse than ever and he had to call their attention to the pictures, tho' what it was all about he couldn't in the least recollect. Thomas seems to me to have become all of a sudden an old man so grey and so quiet. I hope he has found some happy subject to write about, tho' he will hardly get such another so soon as his last. He talked with the greatest composure of Clough starving a little & fighting his way as a literary man. He must have been talking very openly of his literary plans, & Carlyle made him I think a most capital suggestion which he said he had already thought of.[1]

[1] ? Jan. 1852. Clough resigned his position at University Hall in Dec. 1851, expecting to get the classical chair of University College, Sydney. On 2 Jan. he heard he had not got it. Other misfortunes followed. The Carlyles and Macaulay were guests of the Ashburtons in early Jan. 1852. Carlyle's former subject was the biography of his friend John Sterling, and he was still undecided about Frederick.

Robert Chambers, the Edinburgh publisher, called some time in the eighteen-fifties:

> He is a capital fellow something like Macaulay. . . . Naturally Thomas' chief topic was abuse of cheap literature, and really Chambers managed beautifully not understanding Thomas' sailing and that he would come round on the other tack.

Another day, Erasmus drove the Carlyles about

> to leave cards on a variety of grandees. Thomas was graduating for the Athenaeum and spent half the time describing his rheumatism. They had been the night before at a large party at Monckton Milnes which went off rather stiffly as Madame sat in the farthest corner with Florence [Nightingale] & took no charge of her guests & didn't know half of them.
>
> (March 1852)

The letters often reinforce what we already know: that Erasmus, for example, was a support to Jane when Carlyle left for Germany, taking her to see the balloon ascent of her cousin John Welsh, or receiving a visit from her a day or so later to cheer him in the agonies of house-removing. A few days earlier, he had called

> to find her sitting in a corner of the drawing-room the rest being filled with furniture the house in the hands of plasterers and painters the picture of discomfort. She has no maid only a child & can get no dinner so I humanely gave her one today.
>
> (22 Aug. 1852)

Although these details are hardly important in themselves, they suggest a happy intimacy and a continuous to-and-fro visiting which makes Erasmus's judgment of the Carlyles of weight when it comes.

So it goes on, with a visit to Cheyne Row 'to admire Mrs Brookfield but she failed and instead I had one of those frightful Italian German teas with three or four languages mashed into the same sentence'. Or they meet by accident: 'I went to the London Library by way of a mild forest ramble and fell in with Mrs C.'.

In March 1854, 'Being particularly dead on Sunday my fate was to have an endless call from Monkton Milnes & after that from Carlyle and precious dull we were I am conscious'. On 11 August Erasmus went to Chelsea,

> and had a prose with Thomas who was in a very indifferent mood about the war. Ld A[shburton] had just been there . . . but I don't know that I heard anything not in the Times. He said Lord Raglan was everything and had forced on the expedition the French being very unwilling to go, Prince Napoleon saying: it is all very well for you for it will only be a change of ministry but with us a change of dynasty.

That was the day Thomas started his beard and Lord Ashburton put his 'seven razors in his pocket & walked off with them'.

They exchange news of friends: of Colonel Anthony Sterling, at the front in the Crimea, or Mazzini who has fallen out of favour with Jane though not with Fanny. There are a number of gossipy references to Mrs Gaskell, about whom Erasmus seems to have agreed with Jane who wrote to Thomas (12 Sept. 1851)[1] that 'there is an atmosphere of moral dullness about her', whereas Erasmus, after attending a party at which she was present with the young Mrs Ruskin, privately classified them as 'Beauty and the Beast': 'I drank so much champagne . . . that I felt up to a little flirtation with La Ruskina. She came to me in the intervals of waltzing for eau de cologne'. On 10 May 1855 he writes an involved account of how Mrs Gaskell had repeated some scandal about 'Mr Hawkes 2 wives', which seems to have started with Jane and Fanny and which found its way back to Thomas via Mazzini who demanded an explanation. In another letter (of uncertain date), 'Mrs G is getting to be the exact type of Hawthorne's British matron'.

On 26 August ?1857, Erasmus reports: 'Even a tea party is an event with me, & I had one on Sunday, Carlyle coming to me at

[1] NLS:MS, 604.306.

4 to go & dine at the Athenaeum, talking without any flashes of silence till 10'. Possibly about October 1854, even Carlyle's brother John turns to Erasmus: his newly-wedded wife had died, and he may have drifted round to Queen Anne St. soon after this: 'As proof how strong I am', writes Erasmus, who had been dangerously ill himself, 'I bore a long visit today from Dr Carlyle which is more than Mrs C does without swearing, & I have no doubt he is horribly tiresome as a visitor'.

The effect of these minor touches is to humanize the Carlyles, which is badly needed, particularly by Thomas. Not only the respect with which he was regarded in his own day, but the reaction and then the counter-reaction have made him too solemn a figure. Humour was one of his characteristics, exaggeration another, the wish to stimulate by outrage, and to draw analogies so fanciful that they stirred the most torpid to respond. What Carlyle liked in Erasmus was partly his gentle sarcasm; and Carlyle's very outrageousness was what Erasmus found entertaining. He is quick to grumble if Thomas's company fails to enliven. As Carlyle grew older, without the provoking sparkle of Jane, the younger men about him were too reverential. Contradiction might have helped, and mild ridicule worked wonders.

Erasmus's reports continue, and on 19 Oct. 1863 one is to say: 'Mrs C is on the sick list having had a bad fall in the city, she was in bed for a fortnight & looked the picture of weakness on her sofa in her bedroom'. Recovery was slow and, next spring, when she was removed for convalescence, it was to Erasmus that Carlyle turned 'to beg for the carriage next day', though 'she did not use it'.

Clearly we don't have all Erasmus's letters to the Wedgwoods, nor were the Carlyles always in mind when he was writing; but there are signs that he continued to give his support. As Carlyle was labouring through the fourth volume of *Frederick*, for example, Erasmus encouraged him to look for aid to his brother Charles. It happened that Carlyle remembered having read a guidebook about Saxon Switzerland which commented usefully on its geology, and he hoped that the brothers could arrange for the Geological Society to lend him a copy. Erasmus wrote to

Charles, offered his own services, and at last ran it to earth, writing to his brother: 'It is really wonderful the trouble Carlyle takes for such a minute point—I have had 4 or 5 letters & he has probably written half-a-dozen besides'.[1]

Frederick was finished in 1865 and, at the end of March 1866, Carlyle left Jane in Cheyne Row and set off for Edinburgh to be installed as University Rector, on 2 April. He was to return to London via Dumfriesshire; and, on Friday 20 April, Erasmus wrote that he had been with Jane 'a long time . . . & she was extra well'. The next day, as he was to tell the Wedgwoods in some detail on 24 April, she had died: 'How he will carry on his life I can't think'. In fact, Frances and Hensleigh had already heard fully from the wife of the Rector of Chelsea, with the same foreboding: 'How he will bear the blow & the loss, no one can guess— but we *must* fear it for him. Will you let Mr Erasmus Darwin know these few particulars'. That Erasmus helped Carlyle at this time is shown in the last of Carlyle's letters (22 Oct. 1866) that Frances and Hensleigh kept:

> I was sorry to have missed you ag*n*, when you were so good as to call. It is very long since we met; and much has befallen to us all since then!
>
> I w*d* right willingly come on Sat*y* Ev*g*; but alas I must not, I cannot! I have not been out, to dinner or the like, since April last; and feel mostly as I c*d* never go ag*n*; at least, I shudder from it as time yet is. Tell Darwin how faithfully I always remember him, and his unwearied goodness to me, among many sufferings of his own.

It has to be assumed that after Jane's death, if not before, the friendship somewhat fell away, and certainly the record gets patchier. In his memoir of Jane, written straight after her death and given in the *Reminiscences*, Carlyle records that Erasmus's 'visits latterly have been rarer and rarer, health so poor, I so occupied, etc. etc.' But they went on, and the second generation began to be

---

[1] *Frederick* (1864), IV, 595–6 identifies it. ED to Carlyle, 23 June 1862, MS: NLS, 1768.34 and ED to Charles Darwin, late June, 1 and 2 July 1862, MS, Cambridge University Library, refer to the matter.

involved.[1] Erasmus writes to his niece Hope Wedgwood: 'We are very jolly here. . . . Our greatest piece of dissipation was drinking tea at Chelsea when C talked for two hours without allowing us to get a word in and no unpleasant subjects for a wonder' (19 Sep. 1864). On 17 June 1866 Julia Wedgwood writes to her Aunt Rich, when staying with the Erskines, 'They talk here much of Carlyle he said he felt "his existence laid in ruins" on his wife's death bed. They all say they never saw him so sweet & genial as at Edinburgh'. On 2 July she writes again:

> he [Erskine] has been talking a good deal about Carlyle today, he says he thinks C. believes more than he knows that he has found it in his late sorrow quite impossible to avoid the language of religion in speaking to him, & that he always meets with an entire response from C. There was a letter from Dr Carlyle today in which he spoke of his brother as now regularly occupied, & writing a little every day, but he did not say what.

It was the memorial essay on Jane which Froude was to include practically unaltered in the *Reminiscences*, in spite of Carlyle's note on 28 July that *if* published it must not be '*without fit editing*'.

Julia continued to visit Linlathen and when Erskine lost his sight she helped by writing some of his letters, one of which was in reply to Carlyle:

> Your letter was the first thing that roused him to some interest in anything. . . . I have not had anything to read him with which I felt his spirit so much in harmony as your letter. . . . He listens still with the most acute attention to everything I read him. We read a little of 'a day with Friedrich' but he was suffering from the effects of a sleepless night & longing for a soporific so that I turned to some more stupefying reading very soon. . . . It seems impertinent to assure you with what tenderness he speaks of you.
>
> (3 Nov. 1868)[2]

[1] Especially Hope (b. 1844), third daughter of Fanny and Hensleigh; Katherine Euphemia (b. 1839), the second; and Frances Julia, called 'Snow', (1833–1912), the first and eldest child. She contributed to periodicals, wrote novels and various other works, and was the friend and correspondent of Browning.

[2] MS: NLS, Acc. 2712.

No doubt she received a cordial reply, for she was soon confident enough to call on Carlyle in London:

Oh I had such a funny visit to Carlyle this week! Was it not brazen of me to go all by myself? We were he, his little niece & an impudent black cat, who insisted on taking a large share in the conversation. He [not the cat, presumably] began talking about Chopin's music, with such enthusiasm as I did not think was in him, at least about music—he said it was a fountain of exquisite harmony.

(To Aunt Rich, 17 July)

In 1877 Froude persuaded Carlyle to sit for his portrait to Millais, and Erasmus went with a party to see it, reporting to his niece Katherine Euphemia:

Millais having released Carlyle Miss Aitken took a scotch lady to see the picture.[1] She lamented there was no Titian now, & told Millais that his picture was modern & vulgar. He admitted that it was modern, but the other epithet put his back up and he has quoted it to various people, but I did not hear that any one of them was candid enough to endorse the remark.

(12 July 1877)

The record grows sparser as both grew sick and disinclined to write or visit, but there remain one or two notable incidents. On 17 January 1877 *The Times* ran a gossipy news-item:

MR CARLYLE ON THE GOSPEL OF DIRT.—*The Ardrossan and Saltcoats Herald* publishes the following extract of a letter written to a friend by Mr Carlyle:—'A good sort of man is this Darwin, and well meaning, but with very little intellect. Ah, it is a sad, a terrible thing, to see nigh a whole generation of men and women professing to be cultivated, looking around in a purblind fashion, and finding no God in this universe. . . . All things from frog spawn; the gospel of dirt the order of the day. The older I grow . . . the more comes back to me the sentence in the Catechism which I learned when a child, and the fuller

[1] Mrs Anstruther: see D. A. Wilson and D. W. MacArthur, *Carlyle in Old Age* (London, 1934), 405.

and deeper its meaning becomes—"What is the chief end of man? To glorify God and enjoy him for ever". No gospel of dirt, teaching that men have descended from frogs, through monkeys, can ever set that aside.'

Carlyle's response was to send a denial to *The Times* through his friend Mrs Lecky (wife of the historian), using her no doubt because his right hand had long been paralysed; and *The Times* duly recorded it (20 Jan.) A week later he called on Erasmus, who wrote to his brother on 27 January:

Dear Charles

Carlyle was here today & said he hoped you had not been annoyed by that forged letter of his. The little paragraph I sent you was written by Mrs Leckie by his desire. He said the letter expressed just the reverse of his opinion that you were a noble generous good man and your intellect of the highest scientific order. He said he had been bothered to death by the numbers of letters he got on it, 3 yesterday and 1 this very day & he had not heard the last of it. Going down stairs he said give my compliments & say it was an infernal lie.[1]

It has been implied that this was just a tactful withdrawal on Carlyle's part, and that because he had said worse things of Darwinism the truth or falsehood of the denial makes no difference. Yet if Carlyle were a demonstrable liar and self-parodist the difference would be considerable. In fact *The Times* had it wrong: there never was such a letter, but the remarks were supposed to be from an account of Carlyle's conversation given by an American.[2] We can believe this or not, but may prefer to think of Carlyle, at the age of eighty-one, making the effort of a personal call to reassure his friend.

Clearly Erasmus accepted Carlyle's denial and continued to visit.[3] Two years later, Charles Darwin's eldest son William, one

[1] MS, Cambridge University Library. The passage from the *Ardrossan Herald* is given in full by Gertrude Himmelfarb, *Darwin and the Darwinian Revolution* (London, 1959), 248–9.

[2] Thomas Wylie, *Thomas Carlyle, The Man and His Books*, revised Wm. Robertson (London, 1909), 381.

[3] As on 19 July 1878, mentioned in a letter to Euphemia Wedgwood.

of whose greatest pleasures was visiting 'Uncle Eras', wrote to his mother about being taken for a drive with Carlyle, recounting a long conversation which ended: 'As we came away he asked after my father, and said with a grin, "but the origin of species is nothing to me". . . . He talked very easily and without any condescension, or oracularly'.[1]

Carlyle died on 5 February 1881, and Erasmus had the doubtful satisfaction of reading about himself in the *Reminiscences* which Froude put out in the next few weeks. It was mostly made up of the pieces Carlyle had been writing just after Jane's death, when his friends had been anxious about how he would bear the strain. Their sarcasm, bite, and disregard for what some of his readers might think, had no doubt been a relief; and, once written, they were left unrevised either by Carlyle or their nominal 'editor', Froude. Yet Erasmus was probably less concerned about what Carlyle said in them about himself than about his brother. The later Darwins have always expressed mild outrage at Jane's calling Erasmus 'a perfect gentleman' ('obvious') and Thomas's saying that he could often be sardonic ('always kind')[2]; yet apart from this Erasmus was set down as 'one of the sincerest, naturally truest, and most modest of men' and rather preferable to Charles 'for intellect'.[3]

But Erasmus joined many of the Cheyne Row circle in deploring the way Froude had rushed out the unedited *Reminiscences*, with no more consideration for Carlyle's reputation than for the old friends he had savaged in them. He was too unwell to protest, but rejoiced at the prospect of reading what his niece Julia Wedgwood would have to say about them in the *Contemporary Review*:

> I am longing to see Snow's attack upon Froude—according to H. Allen whom I saw today she had done it most thoroughly. The nasty Quarterly is glad that Froude left out nothing so that Carlyle may be effectually lowered in the world's opinion.
>
> (?1 May 1881)

[1] MS, Wedgwood papers, also Litchfield, II,235–7. It is clear that the call was made with Erasmus, the only person able to introduce him and provide a carriage. The letter speaks of 'we' throughout.

[2] Litchfield, II,147.

[3] *Reminiscences*, ed. Froude (1881), II, 207–9.

And again: 'I am delighted with Snow's article and the way she has administered divine vengeance—how he must long to put her in the dock'[1] (9 May 1881).

It is certainly the most scathing, accurate and weighty of the many adverse reviews the book received, the longest and the most authoritative.[2] Julia was already the 'intellectual heavyweight' that E. M. Forster was to call her;[3] she had memories of the Carlyles of her own; her first letter from Jane is dated 1854; and she was at one in her judgment with her uncle and family. Her blame is placed squarely on Froude, and Carlyle excused only as a sick man whose private recollections, written when distraught with grief, came from a 'diseased' mind. All this was obviously welcome to Erasmus, who not only approved her verdict but had long ago confided to the Wedgwoods how he disliked Froude. In 1864 he had written to Fanny about the *Edinburgh Review*'s remarks on volumes v–viii of Froude's *History of England*:

> I think it is very well done, quizzing his folly with not too heavy a touch, and not getting angry with him, which I can hardly avoid, tho' I know his nature can believe nothing except from some oblique point of view. I feel quite sure he never would have been boiled or roasted himself tho' he would have been rather a temptation to an inquisitor.

On another occasion he remarks, 'I can forgive any amount of cruelty to Froude'.

He obviously detested Froude's partisan, protestant, slave-driving jingoism, and he possibly felt that he fostered the same spirit in Carlyle. And Froude may well have been aware of this.

---

[1] See the *Contemporary Review*, 39 (1881), 821–42. Erasmus also comments on Froude's threats about what he might yet have to reveal in the biographical papers he was using, and supposes that Froude thought that they might be used to give 'a very different aspect of the domestic affairs' of the Carlyles 'from the idyllic one now published'. At no point does ED waver from his position of affectionate concern for both partners. In my view he was entirely right and Froude wrong: see also my 'Froude and Carlyle: Some New Considerations', *Carlyle Past and Present*, ed. with R. L. Tarr (1976), 239–69.

[2] It is reprinted in her *Nineteenth Century Teachers* (1909), 156–91.

[3] *Marianne Thornton* (London, 1956), 223.

'To those' Erasmus Darwin 'did not like', writes Mrs. Litchfield, 'and he did not like everyone, his personality, always impressive, might have been awful' (II,147). He may well have foreseen how it would be our misfortune that Froude was able to stamp on the record his own impression of Carlyle, erecting a biographical frontier in the nine volumes of *Reminiscences, Letters and Memorials*, and *Life* which he published in four years, that has hindered us from getting to know the earlier Carlyle.

For the significance of this final incident is that we can see that Froude *did* take his vengeance on the Wedgwoods and Darwin. When he disliked anyone, he just left them out of the record altogether. He did the same with Carlyle's niece, Miss Aitken, with whom Carlyle had lived for the last fifteen years. Neither Erasmus nor Julia's parents are indexed in the *Life*. They are hardly even mentioned. The charm and warmth of their affection is effaced, and a bright aspect of the Carlyles is over-shadowed. Carlyle as Froude describes him is merely Froude's Carlyle; and Froude was the author of an apparently 'official' life sanctioned only by his own opinion and personal vendettas.

Yet Julia was able to write her own account of both the Carlyles and Erasmus in an obituary letter she sent to the *Spectator* (3 Sep. 1881), when her uncle died later in 1881. She began by expressly accepting the portrait in the *Reminiscences*, 'not regretted by any who loved the original', spoke of Erasmus as the man Carlyle 'most loved . . . among those not his kindred', and recalled how when he was ill in 1854 the warmth of Carlyle's affection had been shown by anxious letters to her parents, 'still fresh in my memory'.[1] Charm, repose, a quaint and delicate humour are all said to have made Erasmus Darwin someone that those who knew him remembered 'with the same distinctness as they remember a creation of genius'. These are far from being the qualities we also usually associate with Carlyle: but perhaps we have been wrong, and wrong because we have been misled.

---

[1] Unpublished, but some of those that survive will be introduced into the Duke–Edinburgh edition of the *Collected Letters*, and I hope to write separately about the Carlyles and the Wedgwoods.

VI

The First Setting of Tennyson's 'Morte D'Arthur'

H. A. MASON

Or that deepwounded child of Pendragon
Mid misty woods on sloping greens
Dozed in the valley of Avilion,
Tended by crownèd queens.
The Palace of Art

READERS who first met *Morte D'Arthur* as a closing portion of Tennyson's *Idylls of the King*, and have never consulted the second volume of *Poems* (1842), find it almost impossible to assess the aptness of the lines which in that edition were printed before and after the poem, and give the poem a setting as a traditional ghost-story told in the expiring hour of Christmas Eve. The difficulty is increased if we consult Hallam Tennyson's *Memoir* and ponder the remarks Tennyson made in his old age on his whole Arthurian venture and its gradual (very gradual) progress to completion over the years, for he was clearly unable (or unwilling) to get back to the time of the original composition (*circa* 1834) when his mind was filled with the pain of losing his friend, Hallam. Of course, it may be that at no time was Tennyson clear as to how much he wanted to be included in the many meanings of the poem. At any rate there is no remark of his that helps us to determine the governing idea of the whole poem.

It is therefore helpful to turn to writers who were not blinded by hindsight and had to assess its epic pretentions from the poem and its setting. And it is fair to begin with those who did not know that the 'setting' was a later addition, composed *circa* 1837–1838, a setting which Tennyson had then suppressed when he first had the 1842 volume set up and reprieved at the last minute.

The extreme view that this setting transfigures what was a mere fragment and enables the reader to take the fragment seriously may be found in a contribution to *Cambridge Essays* (1855), where George Brimley concluded:

> The poem justifies itself, by its finished excellence, as a work of art, but it is spiritualized and raised above merely pictorial and dramatic beauty by its setting, and the poet's nineteenth-century point of view.

From this we can see that whatever be the master meaning of the poem, the meaning proclaimed in the setting was among other things an attempt to gratify a contemporary longing. There is no mistaking the readiness of Brimley's response, as a further quotation will show:

> The first poem in the Third Series is called *The Epic*, and contains a fragment on the death of King Arthur, read to the party assembled in a country house at Christmas. Set thus amidst the fire-side talk of Christmas Eve, *Morte d'Arthur* ceases to be a fragment of animated and picturesque epic story, and becomes the answer of a Christian poet to the querulous lamentation of the Christian ritualist and dogmatist over the decay of faith. The noble humanity and piety that shone in chivalry are not dead, he tells us, with King Arthur, though
>
> > The sequel of to-day unsolders all
> > The goodliest fellowship of famous knights
> > Whereof this world holds record.
>
> Excalibur, the mystic sword which Arthur wielded so long and so well, vanishes with him from the world, but the heavenly weapons wherewith men fight the good fight are still bestowed upon the heroes of the successive ages, differing in form and temper, but effective for the various work, and fitted to the hands that are to wield them. Not only has each age its new work to do, its new instruments and new men to do it, as matter of historical fact, but it must be so—
>
> > The old order changeth, yielding place to new,
> > And God fulfils himself in many ways,
> > Lest one good custom should corrupt the world.

The Arthur of the round-table is gone to fable-land; but the desire and hope that gave birth to the legends of chivalry yet live—the dim prophecy that he will one day return and rule over Britain is ever accomplishing itself. What mean those Christmas bells that tell us yearly Christ is born? Do they lie? No! they blend with all noble legends that speak of man's great deeds, of his vaster aspirations, of his yet unaccomplished hopes. They remind us of the prophecy to which fact is tending, of the ideal after which the real is striving. To him whose heart is hopeful and brave, who will not be the slave of formulas, 'Arthur is come again, and cannot die,' is the burden of the world's song; 'Come again, and thrice as fair,' is heard in every change by which the thoughts of men are widened and their hearts enlarged; 'Come with all good things, and war shall be no more,' the strain that echoes clear in the distance, and most clear when the church bells ring in the Christmas morn. *Morte d'Arthur* is no mere story out of an old book, refurbished with modern ornaments, but a song of hope, a prophecy of the final triumph of good.

Further confirmation of the state of mind appealed to in this setting can be obtained from FitzGerald, who knew the poem in its original form, disliked the opening lines of the setting, but took the point of the 'epilogue' to heart, as we may see from several incidental remarks in his dialogue *Euphranor*, which he may have composed as early as 1846, but first published in 1851. For he there refers explicitly to the poem:

As Tennyson says, King Arthur, who was carried away wounded to the island valley of Avilion, returns to us in the shape of a 'modern Gentleman' . . .

and argues that if such a man may possess in contemporary life the 'stateliest port' referred to by Tennyson, it 'will not be due to the Reading-desk or Easy-chair'. What made this forward reference from King Arthur easy was the view that Chivalry was not essentially connected with a remote romantic world but was 'a name for that general Spirit or state of mind, which disposes men to Heroic and Generous actions; and keeps them conversant with all that is Beautiful and Sublime in the Intellectual and Moral world'.

Tennyson, we may therefore hazard, was, in opening this vein, giving grounds for Roscoe's opinion that he was the most *modern* of poets:

His is a mind in exact harmony with the times in which he lives.

Yet among contemporary reviewers there was one who, though very much in sympathy with this second volume of 1842, objected strongly to the prefatory portion, *The Epic*. Leigh Hunt seems to me to have put his finger on something in Tennyson's manner and tone which must be admitted to be there. What he disliked here was more marked in the opening lines of *Godiva*:

> *I waited for the train at Coventry;*
> *I hung with grooms and porters on the bridge,*
> *To watch the three tall spires; and there I shaped*
> *The city's ancient legend into this:—*

but he also objected to the tone of

> 'You know,' said Frank, 'he flung
> His epic of King Arthur in the fire!'
> And then to me demanding why? 'Oh, sir,
> He thought that nothing new was said, or else
> Something so said 'twas nothing. . . .'

which provoked the remark:

this kind of mixed tone of contempt and nonchalance, or, at best, of fine-life phrases with better fellowship, looks a little instructive, and is, at all events, a little perilous. There is a drawl of Bond-street in it.

Leigh Hunt certainly hit the mark in his next sentence; at least as concerns *Morte D'Arthur*:

We suspect that these poems . . . are among those which Mr Tennyson thinks his best, and is most anxious that others should regard as he does. . . .

For the *Memoir* contains a letter of 1834, addressed to one of his close friends, in which Tennyson confessed, 'I myself think [it] the best thing I have managed lately', and a note from FitzGerald:

Resting on our oars one calm day on Windermere, whither we had gone for a week from dear Spedding's (Mirehouse), at the end of May 1835, resting on our oars, and looking into the lake quite unruffled and clear, Alfred quoted from the lines he had lately read us from the MS of 'Morte d'Arthur' about the lonely lady of the lake and Excalibur—

> Nine years she wrought it, sitting in the deeps
> Upon the hidden bases of the hills.

'Not bad that, Fitz, is it?'

It strikes me as one of the signs that the poem is incapable of sustaining the attention of a *thinking* mind (however much it may appeal to the imagination) that nobody has remarked on the impossibility of attaching any meaning to these lines. The contrast with those from which the passage started is instructive. It is first of all worth noting how many of the 'Homeric echoes' in the poem are echoes rather of Pope's translation. If we consult Tennyson's model, we find that the passage from Homer is rooted in sense. Vulcan had been thrown out of heaven by Juno, who could not bear the sight of his deformity. Thetis had kept him out of harm's way in one of her underwater caves. There he exercised his budding talents as a metal worker by fashioning small *objets d'art*.

> Ev'n then, these Arts employ'd my infant Thought;
> Chains, Bracelets, Pendants, all their Toys I wrought.
> Nine Years kept secret in the dark Abode,
> Secure I lay, conceal'd from Man and God:
> Deep in a cavern'd Rock my Days were led;
> The rushing Ocean murmur'd o'er my Head.

But what made the Lady of the Lake feel so *lonely* for nine whole years? And what exactly was she sitting on all that time? Strictly, the only thing that can be *on* the base of a hill is the rest of that hill. And did she have a forge handy? And did she do all the forging sitting down? People who professionally display to visitors the treasures of their museums have been known to talk nonsense. But this explanation of how Excalibur came into being would hardly 'win reverence' from any audience.

The impression of fatuous self-admiration would have been strengthened for Hunt if Tennyson had not struck out before publication some lines of a flattering self-portrait. At one time he had thought of placing them as a prologue to *The Gardener's Daughter*. I quote them to show how close Tennyson's self-admiration came to the adoration he saw in the eyes of his friends.

> Look on those manly curls so glossy dark,
> Those thoughtful furrows in the swarthy cheek;
> Admire that stalwart shape, those ample brows,
> And that large table of the breast dispread,
> Between low shoulders; how demure a smile,
> How full of wisest humour and of love,
> With some half-consciousness of inward power,
> Sleeps round those quiet lips; not quite a smile;
> And look you what an arch the brain has built
> Above the ear! and what a settled mind,
> Mature, harboured from change, contemplative,
> Tempers the peaceful light of hazel eyes,
> Observing all things.

FitzGerald virtually reproduces this passage in *Euphranor*:

For, as King Arthur shall bear witness, no young Edwin he, though, as a great Poet, comprehending all the softer stops of human Emotion in that Register where the Intellectual, no less than what is call'd the Poetical, faculty predominated. As all who knew him know, a Man at all points ... of grand proportion and feature, significant of that inward chivalry, becoming his ancient and honourable race; when himself a 'Yongé Squire,' like him in Chaucer 'of grete strength,' that could hurl the crow-bar further than any of the neighbouring clowns, whose humours, as well as of their betters,—Knight, Squire, Landlord and Land-tenant,—he took quiet note of, like Chaucer himself.

Although FitzGerald went on to include among the 'all things' the poet observed, 'some of those uncertain phenomena of Night: unsurmised apparitions of the Northern Aurora, by some shy glimpses of which no winter—no, nor even summer—night, he said, was utterly unvisited', yet when Tennyson brought them into the poem:

> Shot like a streamer of the northern morn,
> Seen where the moving isles of winter shock
> By night, with noises of the northern sea

it is noteworthy that he did so, as Christopher Ricks was the first to point out, in the language of Walter Scott:

> The Monk gazed long on the lovely moon,
>   Then into the night he looked forth;
> And red and bright the streamers light
>   Were dancing in the glowing north.
> So had he seen, in fair Castile,
>   The youth in glittering squadrons start;
> Sudden the flying jennet wheel,
>   And hurl the unexpected dart.
> He knew, by the streamers that shot so bright,
> That spirits were riding the northern light.

Not all the self-references are fatuous, however. For we have a confession about his habitual heavy drinking, which has, on the whole, been played down by biographers. Yet it is usually supposed that Tennyson was not unwilling to refer to the *manner* in which he read his own verse:

> Read, mouthing out his hollow oes and aes,
> Deep-chested music. . . .

The commentators, quite properly, refer us here to some remarks by FitzGerald:

> Mouthing out his hollow oes and aes, deep-chested music, this is something as A.T. reads, with a broad north country vowel, except the u in such words as 'mute', 'brute', which he pronounces like the thin French 'u'. His voice, very deep and deep-chested, but rather murmuring than mouthing, like the sound of a far sea or of a pine-wood, I remember greatly struck Carlyle when he first came to know him. There was no declamatory showing off in A.T.'s recitation of his verse; sometimes broken with a laugh, or a burlesque twist of voice, when something struck him as quaint or grim.

But since there is a surviving gramophone record of his voice, we ought also to listen to the verdict of Henry James.

> He had not got a third of the way through Locksley Hall, which, my choice given me, I had made bold to suggest he should spout . . . before I had begun to wonder that I didn't wonder, didn't at least wonder more consumedly; as a very little while back I should have made sure of my doing on any such prodigious occasion. I sat at one of the windows that hung over space, noting how the windy, watery autumn day, sometimes sheeting it all with rain, called up the dreary, dreary moorland or the long dun wolds; I pinched myself for the determination of my identity and hung on the reader's deep-voiced chant for the credibility of his: I asked myself in fine why, in complete deviation from everything that would have seemed from far back certain for the case, I failed to swoon away under the heaviest pressure I had doubtless ever known the romantic situation bring to bear. So lucidly all the while I considered, so detachedly I judged, so dissentingly, to tell the whole truth, I listened; pinching myself, as I say, not at all to keep from swooning, but much rather to set up some rush of sensibility. It was all interesting, it was at least all odd; but why

in the name of poetic justice had one anciently heaved and flushed with one's own recital of the splendid stuff if one was now only to sigh in secret 'Oh dear, oh dear'? The author lowered the whole pitch, that of expression, that of interpretation above all; I heard him, in cool surprise, take even more out of his verse than he had put in, and so bring me back to the point I had immediately and privately made, the point that he wasn't Tennysonian. I felt him as he went on and on lose that character beyond repair, and no effect of the organ-roll, of monotonous majesty, no suggestion of the long echo, availed at all to save it. What the case came to for me, I take it—and by the case I mean the intellectual, the artistic—was that it lacked the intelligence, the play of discrimination, I should have taken for granted in it, and thereby, brooding monster that I was, born to discriminate *à tout propos*, lacked the interest.

When we are weighing the force of 'fatuous', we might well put this passage alongside this:

> Sat rapt: it was the tone with which he read—
> Perhaps some modern touches here and there
> Redeem'd it from the charge of nothingness. . . .

If the reference to the bells of Christmas morn assisted the response that, as we have seen, the setting in fact elicited, the reference to Christmas Eve may have been designed to protect the poem from the disgust of a reader who could see no modern application in the treatment of Arthur. Although there are one or two references which are certainly drawn from life, such as the skating on the pond, I take it that there never was such an actual recitation of the poem on Christmas Eve in the years 1835–1838, if only because Tennyson could never have been brought to recite before people who were not already intimate admirers and knew far more of his work than is implied by

> 'we knew your gift that way
> At college; but another which you had,
> I mean of verse (for so we held it then,)
> What came of that?'

I therefore suppose that Tennyson chose the Eve of Christmas as the dramatic occasion somewhat as Shakespeare chose *The Winter's Tale* for a title, for a protection against critics who, like Sterling, found the poem deficient in human interest, and wrote in his review of the 1842 volume:

The miraculous legend of 'Excalibar' [*sic*] does not come very near to us, and as reproduced by any modern writer must be a mere ingenious exercise of fancy.

This supposition is strengthened by the contemporary example of Dickens, who was clearly inspired by Shakespeare to offer his own tale.

Hermione:	Come Sir, now
	I am for you againe: 'Pray you sit by vs,
	And tell's a Tale.
Mamillius:	Merry, or sad, shal't be?
Her.	As merry as you will.
Mam.	A sad Tale's best for Winter:
	I haue one of Sprights, and Goblins.
Her.	Let's haue that (good Sir.)
	Come on, sit downe, come on, and doe your best,
	To fright me with your Sprights: you're powrefull
	at it.
Mam.	There was a man.
Her.	Nay, come sit downe: then on.
Mam.	Dwelt by a Church-yard. . . . .

'Ah!' said the old lady, 'there was just such a wind, and just such a fall of snow, a good many years back, I recollect—just five years before your poor father died. It was a Christmas eve, too; and I remember that on that very night he told us the story about the goblins that carried away old Gabriel Grub.'

If Tennyson had read *The Posthumous Papers of the Pickwick Club* in the years 1836–7, when it had a sensational success, he can hardly

have failed to make a personal application of Chapter XXVIII, and
in particular of these lines:

> How many old recollections, and how many dormant sym-
> pathies, does Christmas time awaken. . . . Many of the hearts
> that throbbed so gaily then, have ceased to beat; many of the
> looks that shone so brightly then, have ceased to glow; the
> hands we grasped, have grown cold; the eyes we sought, have
> hid their lustre in the grave; and yet the old house, the room,
> the merry voices and smiling faces, the jest, the laugh, the most
> minute and trivial circumstance connected with those happy
> meetings, crowd upon our mind at each recurrence of the
> season, as if the last assemblage had been but yesterday!

And if Tennyson did see the book in parts or as a whole, he cannot
have overlooked the scene in the kitchen as illustrated by Phiz:

> 'Our invariable custom,' replied Mr. Wardle. 'Everybody sits
> down with us on Christmas eve, as you see them now—
> servants and all; and here we wait, till the clock strikes twelve,
> to usher Christmas in, and while away the time with forfeits
> and old stories . . .'

While this would suit the fictional setting for the poem:

> At Francis Allen's on the Christmas-eve—
> The game of forfeits done—the girls all kiss'd
> Beneath the sacred bush.

we know something of how the eve was really passed *chez* Tennyson in 1837:

> But let no footstep beat the floor,
>   Nor bowl of wassail mantle warm;
>   For who would keep an ancient form
> Thro' which the spirit breathes no more?
>
> Be neither song, nor game, nor feast . . .

The spirit of Christmas had departed with the death of the father, the loss of the old home, and above all with the death of Hallam. The unmentionable subject of *Morte D'Arthur* was the death of Arthur Hallam. (The suggestion of an epic in twelve books is a pure red herring. Tennyson never at any time had a real subject which could be given epic treatment. The mediaeval Arthur and the body of legends connected with the Round Table had fascinated him when he was a boy and he quite properly saw opportunities in them for poems such as *The Lady of Shalott* and *Sir Launcelot and Queen Guinevere*.) It may therefore be possible that Tennyson felt, as Leigh Hunt put it, 'a certain mixture of timidity and misgiving', about the poem. I do not think that Tennyson saw any of the faults in it which are palpable today. For he, who revised so much, never altered the poem but kept it in print and used it as part of the closing episode in his *Idylls*. But he may have had scruples about it like those which kept him from printing *The Lover's Tale* for so long, although he clearly thought that a good poem for a nineteen-year-old author. Tennyson may have been embarrassed by the revelation in both poems of his *unmanliness* under the shock of sudden deprivation of a loved object:

> *Another*! then it seemed as tho' a link
> Of some tight chain within my inmost frame
> Was riven in twain: that life I heeded not
> Flow'd from me, and the darkness of the grave,
> The darkness of the grave and utter night,
> Did swallow up my vision; at her feet,
> Even the feet of her I loved, I fell,
> Smit with exceeding sorrow unto Death.

Not only did Tennyson feel a comparison with Gethsemane was in place he went on to drag in Golgotha:

> Would I had lain
> Until . . . the wild briar had driven
> Its knotted thorns thro' my unpaining brows. . . .

Now, while it would not be difficult to accumulate further convincing arguments for the view that Tennyson had no serious 'epic' intentions at this date, it is far from obvious that the poem is principally concerned with feelings about the death of Hallam. To bolster the latter case, it might be as well to put it first that in 1842 Tennyson saw the poem as going rather with *Ulysses* and the unpublished *Tithon* than with the 'English Idyls' such as *The Gardener's Daughter*. That is to say, the poem should be regarded as one of his attempts to overcome his unmanly feelings under the shock of Hallam's death by striking the heroic note. To embody the heroic he needed an answerable style. His aim was to put Malory's prose into the equivalent of Homer's verse. It is here of interest to note that several features in the poem that might be excused as carry-overs from Malory were in fact marks of what Tennyson took to be the true Homeric note, as we may see from the following attempt to put Matthew Arnold in his place:

> So Hector said, and sea-like roar'd his host;
> Then loosed their sweating horses from the yoke,
> And each beside his chariot bound his own;
> And oxen from the city, and goodly sheep
> In haste they drove, and honey-hearted wine
> And bread from out the houses brought, and heap'd
> Their firewood, and the winds from off the plain
> Roll'd the rich vapour far into the heaven.
> And these all night upon the bridge of war
> Sat glorying . . .

Tennyson has used 'from out' and 'from off' to plump out the regularity of the iambic pentameter. If we take the opening lines of our poem and compare them with the relevant portion of Malory:

> and thus they fought all the long day, and never stinted till the noble knights were laid to the cold ground; and ever they fought still till it was nigh night, and by that time was there a hundred thousand laid dead upon the down.

we can see that Tennyson was imposing on it his conception of Homer's style:

> So all day long the noise of battle roll'd
> Among the mountains by the winter sea,
> Until King Arthur's table, man by man,
> Had fall'n in Lyonness about their Lord,
> King Arthur. . . .

(which is not so very far off Pope, as here:

> The partners of his fame and toils at *Troy*,
> Around their Lord, a mighty ruin! lye:
> Mix'd with the brave . . .)

The effect of this imposition of an alien manner was to devalue the heroism of Malory's tale and to substitute notes which are both discordant and imperfectly related because the reason for them could never be made explicit. For Arthur cannot be identified with King Arthur nor Tennyson with Bedivere. The real subject, *exposure to and presentation of the death of a beloved object*, suffers from the distraction of pedantic retention of turns from Malory ('and lightly bring me word') and from concentrating our attention on externals, e.g. the noise of armour on rock. Nevertheless many readers have testified to enjoying the poem, not like Brimley as hopeful, but as expressing a decent sadness and melancholy. Tennyson's real subject, however, did not require him to make the two chief figures into human beings. What unique thing Tennyson had to say comes out in the weird lamentations at the passing of Arthur. And the critical point is that, while several of the atmospheric notes seem fussily prominent if we are hungering for a human drama, the general air of waste and loss in the winter landscape powerfully reinforces the central interest, a sense of nightmare, of utter collapse.

It is this which unites the poem with the moments of collapse in *The Lover's Tale*. Here in particular we might recall a sort of pre-vision the young lover had of his ultimate fate:

> With more than mortal swiftness, I ran down
> The steepy sea-bank, till I came upon
> The rear of a procession, curving round

The silver-sheeted bay: in front of which
Six stately virgins, all in white, upbare
A broad earth-sweeping pall of whitest lawn,
Wreathed round the bier with garlands: in the distance,
From out the yellow woods upon the hill
Look'd forth the summit and the pinnacles
Of a gray steeple—thence at intervals
A low bell tolling. All the pageantry,
Save those six virgins which upheld the bier,
Were stoled from head to foot in flowing black. . . .

But while the meaning of this vision is cleared up in the later part
of the story, who can say what happened to Arthur on the lake?
Although I began by dismissing Tennyson's own accounts, there
is one to which I should like now to return:

> The Bishop of Ripon . . . once asked him whether they were
> right who interpreted the three Queens, who accompanied
> King Arthur on his last voyage, as Faith, Hope and Charity. He
> answered: 'They are right, and they are not right. They mean
> that and they do not. They are three of the noblest of women.
> They are also those three Graces, but they are much more. I
> hate to be tied down to say, "*This* means *that*," because the
> thought within the image is much more than any one interpre-
> tation.'

It was thoughts such as these that led me to speak of the poem's
many meanings. I yield with great reluctance to the suggestion,
first put forward by Paden, that long before Tennyson succumbed
to Malory, he had allowed himself to be captivated by books of
comparative mythology which attempted to create a unity of the
principal myths of the great civilizations of the past, and in particular, to the work of G. S. Faber, *The Origin of Pagan Idolatry*,
who saw one fundamental myth repeated in all mythologies, the
myth of a mysterious boat floating on a mysterious lake or ocean
and carrying a hero out of one life and into another, a myth
best known to Bible readers in the story of Noah, but a Noah
interpreted to make it possible to see Arthur as a mythological
figure distinct from the much later 'historical' King and virtually

identical with Osiris and many other god-heroes who die and
return.

I have resisted this suggestion so long not out of obstinacy but
because I could not see that any part of our Tennyson text shows
direct debts to any phrase in *The Origin of Pagan Idolatry*. It is true
that Faber is always referring to islands floating *on the bosom* of a
deep lake, or the Stygian abyss, but that may be a mere coincidence, even when Faber substitutes for islands rafts or barges.
What seems irresistible is the evidence that at one point Tennyson was following Faber's paraphrase of Malory rather than
Malory himself. Here first is the Malory Tennyson knew:

And then he threw the sword into the water as far as he might,
and there came an arm and a hand above the water, and met
it and caught it, and so shook it thrice and brandished. And then
the hand vanished away with the sword in the water.

And here is Faber:

He casts the noble blade into the midst of the stream: when lo,
ere it touches the water, a hand and arm is seen to grasp it, to
flourish it thrice in the air, and then to sink with it beneath the
waves.

It seems likely that from this Tennyson took suggestions for

And fling him far into the middle meer

and

But ere he dipt the surface

and, less probably,

and drew him under in the meer.

What is maddening to the rational enquirer, the superimposi-
tion of innumerable figures over any one chosen myth-hero,
suited Tennyson. So we may include in our imagination all the

females mentioned by Faber as receiving Arthur, from 'the three Guiniveres' to a three-fold representation of the 'female principle', yes, to the White Goddess herself! For this habit allowed Tennyson to envisage this central event in Arthur's story as the central event for mankind, when the whole world perished, in the flood, and its revival depended on the hero's successful death and resurrection. In the Mysteries enacting this event, as students of the Druids proclaimed, for whom the hero-god was Arthur, the 'piercing shrieks', as Faber puts it, from the barge had a particularly poignant meaning, for it was lamentation over the deaths of all those companions of Arthur who were drowned in the attempt to board the mystic barge with him, and thus failed to accompany him through his ordeal and share in his resurrection.

In some such way, then, we may imagine Tennyson coming to find this remarkable embodiment for his sense of 'the very heart of loss'. Tennyson had every right to be proud of these lines, where we experience the rich stores of his imagination connecting the terrors of the child with the adult terrors of the forsaken:

> . . . all the decks were dense with stately forms
> Black-stoled, black-hooded, like a dream . . .
>   and from them rose
> A cry that shiver'd to the tingling stars,
> And, as it were one voice, an agony
> Of lamentation, like a wind, that shrills
> All night in a waste land, where no one comes,
> Or hath come, since the making of the world . . .

VII

Hardy's Poetical Metonymy

JOHN BAYLEY

IN a poetic context the function of anthropomorphism, and its associated rhetorical modes, has always been to help bring together the poet and his reader in a more or less familiar manner with whatever aspects of the natural world are being written about. It is significant that even a parody of the process, like Pope's

> Apply thine engine to the spungie door
> Set Bacchus from his glassy prison free,

only accentuates, to a pleasantly laughable degree, the social function of a poem of animism and metonymy. When Milton writes in Comus

> The sounds and seas, with all their finny drove
> Now to the moon in wavering morrice move

he unites the world of created nature in a dance in harmony with the social aspect of the masque, its audience and performers. When Wordsworth says

> And O, ye Fountains, Meadows, Hills, and Groves,
> Forebode not any severing of our loves!

he suggests the possibility of a break in the relation, which confirms that its existence is assumed by all of us in such a context of diction and feeling.

The congruence of assumption about animated nature seems to be suggested by the form itself, rather than by its specific meaning addressed to us. This could be illustrated from the magnificent

poem by Wilfred Owen, from which his mother cut out a line
and a half to quote on his gravestone.

> Shall Life renew these bodies? Of a truth,
> All death will he annul, all tears assuage?—
> Or fill these void veins full again with youth,
> And wash, with an immortal water, Age?
>
> When I do ask white Age, he saith not so:
> 'My head hangs weighed with snow.'
> And when I hearken to the earth, she saith:
> 'My fiery heart shrinks, aching. It is death.
> Mine ancient scars shall not be glorified.
> Nor my titanic tears, the seas, be dried.'

'Shall life renew these bodies? Of a truth, All death will he annul'
became Lieutenant Owen's epitaph. His poem has a grandeur
which would seem something merely preserved and pretentious
in any other poet of the time, but which Owen has made alive and
his own, his genius infusing something homely into the grandeur,
into the image of Age, and the pathos of the short heavy line he
utters. Poetically this rhetoric, as practised by him, means that the
nature of the replies received from Earth and from Age do not in
any very fundamental sense matter. The poem *Asleep*, about a
dead soldier, asks the same kind of question—'Whether his deeper
sleep lie shaded by the shaking/Of great winds and the thoughts
that hung the stars . . . Or whether yet his thin and sodden head/
Confuses more and more with the low mould'—a question resolved in the line—'Who knows? Who hopes? Who troubles?
Let it pass'. Feeling that can rise to the sublime in this way is not
concerned what lies outside its own mode of expression. Owen's
mother was in a sense justified in making the poem read as she
did, as was Owen himself in his hero-worship of the military
fraternity in whose exploit he died. His poems celebrate war in
the same breath that they proclaim the senseless pity of it, and this
is due in large part to the way he handles his modes of personification and metonymy.

I should like to suggest that Hardy is very much the odd man out in the extensive use he makes of such devices; and that it is this more than anything which determines our sense of the personal and the original in his poetry. He would have enjoyed Owen's poem too; he would have responded both to the sentiment and the personality. But it is very different from any of his own. In its use of the properties it is part of this surprisingly coherent and continuing tradition, a tradition of *understanding*—in Tolstoy's use of the word as a kind of family *rapport*—between the poet and his audience and his poem.

We find it in Auden, who often exaggerates and sends it up, while making use of it.

> Look, stranger, on this island now
> The leaping light for your delight discovers.

The first two words, which have become so well known, and to which everyone responds, again suggest their opposite. The stranger is not a stranger in this poem, and the 'leaping light' is joining with the poet to welcome and please him. In *Musée des Beaux Arts* Auden makes the conviviality one of intellectual agreement, as between poet and reader. The poem succeeds through the clarity and certainty with which it makes us believe that great art demonstrates the *lack* of human solidarity and the indifferent separateness of things in the physical world. But, like Breughel and 'the old masters', the poem makes true of art what it holds to be untrue of life. In the physical world the sun shines 'as it has to'; and for the ploughman the fall of Icarus was not 'an important failure'; but one way in which art achieves its harmony and solidarity is to point out that these are not aspects of the natural world, as the poem does, or by displaying it pictorially, as the poem says the pictures do.

The upshot or end-effect of animistic poetry is thus surprisingly uniform, animism being a sign of the way the poetry is working, rather than of the poet's attitude to the natural world. These sorts of metaphor and metonymy are not particular about their metaphysical status provided they can do their work in the poem. What Frost calls, writing of a field vanishing under snow, having 'no expression, nothing to express', is not possible: the idea of vacancy becomes just as anthropomorphic in his poem as any kind of possession.

The poet's awareness of anthropomorphism, even his deliberate rejection of it, does not stop it operating. The organization and concentration of poetry on the natural order produce a predictable result. The mastery and ecstasy of Hopkins's Windhover is asserted with all the poet's intense individuality; but it is in a harmonious tradition of theology and art, each participant in nature proclaiming 'For this I came'. D. H. Lawrence's homage to his Fish is based on the opposite assertion—'I didn't know his God'—but the fish becomes a creature to be gazed on with fascination and reverence for that reason, as the worshipper of an unknown god. One would suppose that a modern poet like Ted Hughes would have successfully de-anthropomorphized the creatures he looks at, but a style that concentrates on focusing the object as sharply as possible in its vision creates also its own pattern of metonymy, one in which the natural order functions with its own kind of intent and joyless absorption.

Hardy's poetry conspicuously lacks this concentration: and it lacks also the button-holing of the reader that goes with it. One might say that the effect of his anthropomorphic inventions is to suggest that he takes their literalness for granted. It seems as natural that the bodies under the yew roots in the churchyard should be heard to say

> That no God trumpets us to rise
> We truly hope

as it is for a parson's words to pass into the air at a funeral 'with a sad but unperturbed cadence'. Personifying has the truth of a routine rather than of making a point. It is not a question of anything like 'the sun shone as it had to', because the sharp focus achieved by such a perception is absent. The elements of Hardy's awareness and of his handling of language often seem to wander away from each other, not caring—except in point of appearances—whether a point has been established, a poem achieved, or not.

This should be a recipe for bad poetry. Not, as is self-evident, in Hardy's case. Take *The Convergence of the Twain*. The ship, like a human being, has a mate prepared for it; they are 'growing up' together. The twin entities, Titanic and iceberg, are also animate actors, being groomed for their role. But they are *too* animated. The poetic convention of making things into people is used with a degree of homeliness and literalness which overturns its proper function. In all Hardy's work the intersection of place and event is the real basis of its imaginative hold over us. But such intersections do not bring things together in any of the meaning-ful senses which poetic metonymy normally works in aid of. *The Convergence of the Twain* leaves us I think, with a sense not of design but of incalculability, of the separation of each from each. And this is true of the world in which Hardy's spirit moves, absorbed in events, meetings and places which have no real rela-tional aspect. There is only, as it were, a *commemorated* one: the place where X met Y; the point on the stream where there was once a mill; the cliff above the atlantic at Vimiero where on a cer-tain hot afternoon Wellington's troops repulsed the French; the exact aspect of a big ship of war, visible for an hour or so from Portland Bill as she passed down-channel. Hardy's devotion to records reveals a consciousness dedicated to single happenings. His vision of iceberg and Titanic exaggerates the poetic device to the point where it seems to dissolve the understanding between all of us which it was designed to uphold.

The distance which Hardy always keeps from us, the most effec-tive cause of whatever sense we may have of his oddness, makes his use of poetic trope all the more idiosyncratic. The use made of coincidence in his novels has a rather similar role, seeming as it does to exert a pressure that is random and arbitrary, rather than any relation of cause and effect, character and environment. The man who steps at a certain moment from a wood out on to a deserted road is as significant in terms of the record of things as is the gargoyle whose jet of rain water washes away the flowers newly planted on a grave.

Hardy is not only habitually at a distance from us, perhaps unaware of us: we might also say that the perceiver in him has no awareness of the rhetorician and craftsman. In both poems and novels the text can be rather like the pictorial composition that Auden discusses in *Musée des Beaux Arts*—a landscape whose constituent elements are in calm isolation from each other, though appearing as a total composition to viewer or reader. With Hardy it is the methods of composition themselves which appear to pay no attention to each other, and—to adapt his own observation about the cry of a bird at night—to pass into the text without mingling with it. They seem, in the same way, to enter the reader's consciousness without recognizing the intention of doing so. Collusion between poet and reader, elsewhere a constant factor in anthropomorphic metonymy—almost its purpose—is notably absent.

This is what goes on, it seems to me, in three little *jeux d'esprit* about birds. Hardy several times tried out an ingenious version of the triolet in which the repeat line is manoeuvred into changes of sense by means of pause and punctuation.

> Around the house the flakes fly faster
> And all the berries now are gone
> From holly and cotone-aster
> Around the house. The flakes fly—faster
> Shutting indoors that crumb-outcaster
> We used to see upon the lawn
> Around the house. The flakes fly faster,
> And all the berries now are gone.

In another, a rook and a pigeon in a frosty field outside Casterbridge discuss their chances of finding something to eat. In a third, a vilanelle, a thrush who has been caught and caged hopes to learn from men 'how happy days are made to be'. But, when escaped back to the other birds he has to report that this secret

> 'Eludes great man's sagacity
> No less than ours. O tribes in treen!
> Men know but little more than we
> How happy days are made to be.'

There is a portable ambiguity in the refrain—by and for whom are days made to be happy?—which shows how Hardy as craftsman enjoys the verbal evasions of the verse form. The unmistakable Hardyan feature of the poems is the independence the talking birds have from the conventions of the medium which is operating. Hardy literalizes anthropomorphism, as he does coincidence, to the point where it disintegrates without protest into separate ingredients—the life of birds, the life of men, the ingenuities of a poet.

Though we may feel that some are a great deal better than others, Hardy's poems give the impression of being all the same quality where he was concerned. Lack of pretension here goes with his privacy, his distance from us. *The Darkling Thrush*, that 'much admired poem on the century's end', as he called it in the *Life*, is just the same sort of poem as the three little ones about the birds. It needs to be quoted, since my argument requires looking at in some detail.

> I leant upon a coppice gate
>   When Frost was spectre-gray,
> And winter's dregs made desolate
>   The weakening eye of day.
> The tangled bine-stems scored the sky
>   Like strings of broken lyres,
> And all mankind that haunted nigh
>   Had sought their household fires.
>
> The land's sharp features seemed to be
>   The Century's corpse outleant,
> His crypt the cloudy canopy,
>   The wind his death-lament.
> The ancient pulse of germ and birth
>   Was shrunken hard and dry
> And every spirit upon earth
>   Seemed fervourless as I.
>
> At once a voice arose among
>   The bleak twigs overhead
> In a full-hearted evensong
>   Of joy illimited;

An aged thrush, frail gaunt, and small,
    In blast-beruffled plume,
Had chosen thus to fling his soul
    Upon the growing gloom.

So little cause for carolings
    Of such ecstatic sound
Was written on terrestrial things
    Afar or nigh around,
That I could think there trembled through
    His happy good-night air
Some blessed Hope, whereof he knew
    And I was unaware.

Hardy used to notice such things, and in such a woodland scene the deadest winter feature is the light brown tangle of wild clematis, 'Old Man's Beard'—with even its last feathery tufts diminished to nothing by the gales and the frost. This emblem of the dead season is of the most unromantic sort, but it is as positive in its own way as the image of the broken lyre-strings. Nothing could be more characteristic of Hardy than this very fancy image suggested by the very scruffy reality. Shelley, his favourite poet when young, was probably in Hardy's mind.

Make me thy lyre, even as the forest is.

The image of lyres, broken and silenced in the winter of the year—and of the mind and heart?—seems to ignore entirely the physical reality of the Old Man's Beard, and yet to be in peaceable contiguity with it. Hardy mentions the same creeper, but probably in its summer garb, in an equally unexpected place, the poem called *A Procession of Dead Days*, in which he imagines past days coming to visit him in a procession, each bringing what made it memorable.

Enters the day that brought the kiss:
He brought it in his foggy hand
To where the mumbling river is,
    And the high clematis . . .

It is a poem of extraordinary happiness, its feeling of intimacy and delight available to the reader but not pressed upon him. Like the bine-stems and the broken lyres, the literalness of the image, and what it conveys, work by not bothering about each other—the day that brings a kiss in his foggy hand seems able to perform the office in a benevolent way without concerning itself with the nature of the gift or the place to which he brings it, accurately localized as these are.

Hardy's images and realities go about their business in the same preoccupied fashion. He once noted that someone had said country folk did not distinguish between things and persons, and he added that this was also true of the poet. With him there is the same absence of distinction between fact and metaphor. This appears in *The Darkling Thrush* with the arrival of the century's corpse, complete with burial-place and mourners. 'Outleant' is eccentric even by Hardy's standards. A corpse cannot itself lean on anything—only lie—but its stiffness could *be* leant, against a gate for instance. If a rhyme were found, the word 'outlaid' would produce the proper metonymic association with the defunctive image in the two lines that follow, but it would be much less arresting. For the century's corpse, when one comes to think of it, is leant in a reflective pose, much in the way that Hardy himself is. It is the most bizarre of all Hardy's non-recognitions—poet and century contiguous yet quite separate.

Metaphor and descriptive statement are used in apposition, so that each ignores the other, instead of being complementary. The thrush's song is the climax of this tendency, and the thrush himself, 'frail, gaunt and small', its leading man. The metaphors are now religious, and alongside the appearance of the thrush himself, perched by the broken lyres of the woodbine, we fall into something like the progression and cadence of a church hymn. But the 'blessed hope' appropriate to a hymn is unaware of the song the bird himself is singing—its 'happy goodnight air'. The unexpectedness of that line brings tears to the eyes, I think because it introduces a further element into the poem, suggesting something gentle outside its metrical sobriety. The difference is between the sober 'joy' of evensong, based on the hopes and consolations of institutional religion, and the unconnected irresponsible gaiety of a dance, the lively fiddle tunes like 'Haste to the Wedding' and 'The Soldier's Joy', which the youthful Hardy had often played. And such a dance looks for nothing beyond the pleasure of the moment.

It is because the pathetic fallacy is so complete that the thrush and his song remain so wholly outside it. But there is certainly no trace of conscious intention about this—if Hardy could be suspected of any deliberate irony the poem would not be what it is. John Berryman, Donald Davie, and other critics, have variously suggested that Hardy *is* being ironic here; not least by emphasizing in his quiet way what readers of *The Times* would like to hear on the last day of 1900. But this is to bring him into that relation with the reader which other anthropomorphic poets may need and solicit but which just does not seem to occur to Hardy. Nothing in the poem shows the intuitive grasp of the audience which would be needed to organize its constituents for the purpose of such irony. From his comment in the *Life*, indeed, it would seem that the widely favourable response of *bien pensant* readers had not only pleased Hardy but a good deal surprised him, coming as it did at a time when he had resolved not to 'stand up and be shot at' any more by the critics of his last novels. Donald Davie imagines *The Times* readers' gratification at supposing Hardy to be saying: 'I, the well-known atheist and author of *Jude the Obscure*, feel quite humbled by the blessed hope voiced by this bird.' A nice idea, but whatever the readers may have thought there can be no doubt Hardy had nothing like that in mind, and indeed—and as usual—nothing in mind with regard to the reader at all.

The poem itself shows this. It is not conscious of what might be taken as a piously comfortable hope, for Hardy's motives do not recognize each other or the reader, any more than do the separate elements of his poetry and novels. It is certainly paradoxical that by taking anthropomorphism so literally and so much for granted Hardy should seem harder to interpret than a poet who is using it traditionally; and this is why critics read him in such different ways. His straightforwardness seems to isolate him from the reader's expectations in a way no amount of sophistication could do. Such simplicity can exaggerate the impossibility of what the poem presents as literal. The first poem he records as writing, about sixteen years old, is about the Bockhampton cottage and its flora.

> Wild honeysucks
> Climb on the walls, and seem to sprout a wish
> (If we may fancy wish of trees and plants)
> To overtop the appletrees hard by.

The diction and thought go back through Wordsworth to the eighteenth century, but in Hardy the fancy sprouts with primitive force. Wordsworth draws the flowers and ourselves into an area of feeling where emphasis ('I must think, do all I can/That there was pleasure there') conduces to general agreement. Hardy's awareness of the flowers puts them outside the thought he then tacks on, exhibiting—voluntarily or involuntarily—its irrelevance to the flowers themselves. The effectiveness of *The Darkling Thrush*, as we have seen, is that it does not matter what is felt about the bird, it being so obviously outside any such feeling, as the bine-stems are from the broken lyres they suggest.

The same happens in his musing on the lady of *The Sunshade*, which the poet finds as 'a naked sheaf of wires' in the crevice of a cliff.

> Is the fair woman who carried that sunshade
> A skeleton just as her property is,
> Laid in the chink that none may scan?
> And does she regret—if regret dust can—
> The vain things thought when she flourished this?

The point is that dust can't; and that is how the poem makes its mark. In a not wholly dissimilar way Hardy was misunderstood, and the President of the Immortals caused a furore, when he was said to have finished his sport with Tess. The point is that he could not have had any sport with Tess, but Hardy's literal fancy saw him doing it, and enjoying it, like all *fonctionnaires*. Hardy's fancy of things, existing tranquilly alongside the way things are, like one cow beside another in a field, was bound to cause mis-understanding.

So is his very unpretentiousness, which misunderstanding can make to look portentous. To make up the President of the Immortals by a literal translation of Aeschylus, 'the spinner of the years', 'the spirits ironic' and all the rest of them, was only to extend the world his imagination had always made up in poetry —ghosts, birds, dogs, trees, the bodies in their coffins and the dust on the chancel floor—all speaking in their separate functions and not joined in one motion and spirit; made free by his musings but not taken over in them. They are as natural to his world as the rustics of his novels, and have the same air of representing nothing except their own selves. Hardy calls them up and peoples his experience with them: he does not own them. If he did he could share them with us more easily, but as it is they keep themselves to themselves, a stance more social than intellectual. Here again he seems very far away from the intellectual fellowship of Words-worth and Coleridge, and the pantheists and positivists of the nineteenth century. 'All thinking things, all objects of all thought' were not by him impelled with one motion and spirit—very much the opposite. In 1890, at the age of fifty, Hardy wrote in his diary: 'I have been looking for God fifty years, and I think that if he existed I should have discovered him. As an external person-ality, of course—the only true meaning of the word.'

As an external personality—that was indeed for Hardy the only true meaning of the word. God should exist in the same sense as the thrush and the winter's day, the years and the fields. And indeed he *did* exist for Hardy in the same sense as the conscious efforts of the honeysuckles, or the conscious thoughts of the skeleton of the lady of the sunshade. That is to say his imagination worked in alliance with the only God he was prepared to conceive of, but could not believe in.

In the history of lost faith Hardy has a unique place. He has been patronized for his inability to do what other artists and thinkers did who had lost theirs—intellectualize, moralize, build new theo-logies. While he seems almost to parody anthropomorphism he is really going back past its nineteenth-century manifestations to a much simpler version. He does not believe in God, but his imagination believes in everything else, in the way that God was once believed in. He must have shocked many of his readers by the smallness of the change he made. The dead do not take on a different status with the loss of belief in God, but remain as they were in the days of belief, awaiting the resurrection while hoping it won't come. Such a vision of the dead was as uncontemporary at the time as the old idea of them waiting for the Last Trump. This must have riled conventional Christians by taking the business of bodily resurrection more literally than they were accustomed to do, while to high-minded non-believers it must have seemed a grotesque notion expressed with inappropriate intensity.

The strange mixture of belief in all his figments—in their 'externality'—and the literalism which contradicts it ('..if regret dust can') does more than anything, I suspect, to isolate Hardy in his own world, and away from the reader, who, naturally enough, wants to know how seriously Hardy himself takes all this, and what his real attitudes are. In prefaces and elsewhere Hardy himself often professed that he was being funny, and expressed regret that this was not better understood by reviewers and others. I feel myself that the answer is that Hardy was not psychologically prepared to have an audience, even though he wanted to publish his poems; and that this determines the nature of his poetry and how we respond to it and love it, if we do.

I think this can be shown by mentioning Philip Larkin and his admiration for Hardy: such a poem of his as *Church Going* seems very much akin to Hardy, but its success in fact depends on a totally different tone. This concentrates in the word 'serious'—'a serious house on serious earth it is'—describing the instinct which still attracts people to a church, and is no more than 'what remains when disbelief has gone'—when even a need to reject religion no longer counts. The poem is faintly ironic about this reaction and yet wholly sympathetic to it, a combination in its quiet way highly collusive with the reader and rather flattering to him. In the metre and cadence there are echoes of *The Scholar Gipsy*, also a collusive poem with a wry and humorous note in it. We are drawn into higher intimacy with Larkin, as with Arnold; all kindred souls together in this particular kind of seriousness, which of course never takes itself too seriously. Hardy's tone is quite different: it is earnest without being serious, and this makes no comparable appeal to us, though we may come to find it all the more congenial for that.

If Hardy does not try to persuade readers into any kind of intimacy, they are certainly conscious how much he feels it with his own creations, whether it is the thrush, or the rocks whose

> record in colour and cast
> Is—that we two passed.

or Tess herself. Nothing reveals this more than one of his most uncompromisingly simple animistic poems, and by common consent one of his best—*After a Journey*. Hardy's sense of his own wife here as a ghost, taking him on a journey to her old haunts, is so absorbed and intimate as completely to exclude the reader. Like the water moving invisibly under the cliff she communes with him, a great deal more fully than what seems to have taken place 'from forty years ago', in life. What is so moving about these poems is that though the poet is so absorbed in the experience, which excludes us, we can apprehend—all too straightforwardly —how common that experience is. For the bereaved to talk to the one who has gone, and talk more freely than in life, must be as common for human beings as it is rare for them to be able to make it into such poetry.

Hardy makes explicit here what is tacitly taken for granted in so many poems—the indifference between things. 'Ignorant of what there is flitting here to see', its former haunts are unaware of the spirit. Nature is not 'heartless, witless', as in Housman's poem, but simply absorbed in its multiple doings, as Hardy in his memory. The paradoxical literalness of 'if regret dust can' is here wholly naturalized in a touching emotion.

> Trust me, I mind not, though Life lours,
> The bringing me here; nay, bring me here again!

He is there in fact. A real person has invited him, at whatever inconvenience to himself, and will he hopes invite him again. In what seems to him a dialogue he claims that he is

> . . . just the same as when
> Our days were a joy, and our paths through flowers.

He cannot be just the same, any more than the spirit can be summoning him, or the dust can regret. If Hardy were thinking of the reader at all he could hardly say it, yet it is wholly true of the scene inside his imagination.

For his poetry asserts two kinds of truth equally literally, and in the knowledge that they can never be at one with each other. In another and equally memorable poem of the time, *His Visitor*, the ghost is imagined walking across to the house from Mellstock—Hardy does not need to record that she was buried in the churchyard there. But the house has been altered by a new regime.

> So I don't want to linger in this re-decked dwelling,
> I feel too uneasy at the contrasts I behold,
> And I make again for Mellstock to return here never,
> And rejoin the roomy silence and the mute and manifold
> Souls of old.

The visitor will be seen no more in the house, only in the churchyard, which is Hardy's way of saying, not at all. His animism implies the freedom of the spirit to make what it can out of the world it finds itself in, and also that consciousness was not made for that world. Hardy was always a dualist; and in a facetious poem written towards the end of his life he recorded that Dualism was 'a tough old chap'; and all his anthropomorphic devices, however extravagant, reinforce that opinion. There was no single mystery which consciousness might at least aspire to pluck out, like Tennyson's 'flower in the crannied wall'. Revisiting St Juliot at the behest of Emma's ghost brings her closer to him than in the flesh. But even poetic device also knows that dust can't regret, that in truth the phantom inviter now 'nor knows nor cares for Beeny', nor those haunts for her; whatever freedom art gives the *anima* to imagine him, God cannot exist as an external personality, or we should have found him by now.

To speak of 'the modern' merely invites the question of what is meant by it, still more so if the word suggests we have got things right now, and have a better idea of our situation than our forebears did. None the less there is a definable sense in which Hardy today seems a more modern poet than Eliot, or than Auden. His poems may seem closer to the daily situation as we apprehend and feel it. For what is sometimes thought of as the quaintness or outlandishness of Hardy, nowhere more evident than in his poetic animism and metonymy, overlays an attitude which has forsaken the past more decisively than that of any other poet of the time. He commemorates and remembers, because the past has gone for good. But of course his poetry does not advertise this—as Eliot for example stylizes the sterility of the modern age and the refuge in the tradition of faith. It is here that the old-fashioned simplicities of Hardy are at their most effective. He does not want to offer us understanding, or to meet us in the kind of atmosphere which gives an impression of it. But he never made up his mind (as he remarks that Matthew Arnold always seemed to have done) and he never ceased to wish for a way to the better. In the only pages of the *Life* not written by him, his second wife records that he asked in his last hours for Browning's *Rabbi Ben Ezra* to be read to him, and that during the reading his face expressed a great wistfulness. In his poetry wistfulness and modernity, like so many other things, can go regardless of each other and yet side by side.